METAMORPHIC

METAMORPHIC

21st century poets respond to Ovid

edited by
Nessa O'Mahony
and
Paul Munden

RECENT
WORK
PRESS

Metamorphic: 21st century poets respond to Ovid
Recent Work Press
Canberra, Australia

Copyright © the authors, 2017

ISBN: 9780648087847 (paperback)

A catalogue record for this
book is available from the
National Library of Australia

Cover illustration: © Kim Sharkey, 2017
Cover design: Recent Work Press
Set in Baskerville

recentworkpress.com

This book was made with the support of:

The International Poetry Studies Institute,
CCCR, Faculty of Arts and Design,
University of Canberra
www.ipsi.org

for
Clare Elizabeth Mallorie Munden
7/7/59-7/10/17

CONTENTS

BOOK II

BOOK III

BOOK IV

BOOK V

BOOK VI

BOOK VII

BOOK VIII

BOOK IX

BOOK X

BOOK XI

INTRODUCTION

In AD 17, Publius Ovidius Naso, the Roman poet Ovid, died in exile in the Black Sea port of Tomis (now Constanta in Romania). He had offended the emperor, Augustus, for verses that may have touched on scandals in the imperial court, from which he was dismissed in AD 8. Famously grief-stricken, he burnt his manuscript of what would become one of the world's most celebrated anthologies of verse tales.

That work was *Metamorphoses*, which survived because his friends circulated their copies of it. Written in 15 books and with a cast of more than 200 gods, goddessess, nymphs, fauns, men and women, it was a complete history of the world, from creation up to the present day. It was also a study of flux and shifting identity, of power applied and misapplied.

Two thousand years after Ovid's death, we are tempted to think that the celebrated poet might have approved of how this new book, *Metamorphic*, came about.

It began with a status update by Nessa O'Mahony on Facebook, surely the 21st century version of the Roman Forum in terms of gossip spread, political scandal discussed and general chatter shared.

Learned over the weekend that it's the 2,000th anniversary of the Roman poet, Ovid. What say anyone to a 21st century version of Metamorphoses .... poems that incorporate the concept of physical transformation in some way? I've no idea if any publisher would want to publish such an anthology... but I'd love to have a go at putting one together. Any of my poet friends out there interested?

That stray thought, on the desirability of celebrating Ovid's anniversary with a new anthology, got an immediate and enthusiastic response from the many poets on her friends list. One of those, Paul Munden, made the offer to co-edit and help find a publisher. Recent Work Press was ready and willing. Suddenly, the project became a real one.

i

When we put out the initial call for contemporary responses to this ancient text, many of the poets approached expressed their fondness for *Metamorphoses* and the influence that versions of it had had on their work—Ted Hughes's *Tales of Ovid* was mentioned several times, as was Michael Hoffman and James Lasdun's anthology *After Ovid*. In the end, 100 poets from around the world answered our call for new poems that responded to, or revisioned, *Metamorphoses*.

The brief was flexible. They could write new versions of Ovid's original, or they could write poems that simply took the original text as a starting point. Many re-imagined Ovid's stories; others found analogues in other cultures, ancient and contemporary, including accounts of death squads in the Philippines, mothers-and-baby homes in Ireland, social media morality tales, or Chinese legend. The result is a fascinating mix of voices, styles and forms, from the UK, Ireland, Italy, South Africa, India, Singapore, the Philippines, Japan, China, Australia, New Zealand, the US and Canada.

The Facebook post was on 24 April 2017. Six months later the book went to print.

What is clear from the poems contained in this anthology is that the idea of metamorphoses is as significant now as it was in Ovid's time. If we have learnt anything in this somewhat extraordinary first 17 years of the 21st century, it is that nothing remains constant. Public discourse is dominated by transformation, as our understanding of what is true and what is not is constantly turned on its head. Old certainties have been discarded, and the pervasive atmosphere of constant change requires new responses and new ways of navigating a world we no longer recognise. We are in a state of flux, as these poems so memorably demonstrate.

That sense of flux has been sharpened by the plight of refugees, and politicians' outrageous labelling of news as 'fake' to suit their own distorted view of reality. These same politicians have also been party to the resurgent maltreatment of minorities and a rekindling of misogyny. Versions of Ovid's tales of cruelty to women are presented here with considerable force.

Inevitably, there is a renewed questioning of how and why gods should affect human thinking and experience. Part of our current political anguish is driven by religious difference, while at the same time, it is clear that humans are exerting an unprecedented level of influence over Earth's evolution, in what is frequently classified as the Anthropocene epoch. This collection of work responds to these challenges with light and dark, comedy and tragedy; and an insistently contemporary idiom, arresting in its application to the ancient stories. Some poets have gone so far as to use the terminology and textual characters of Twitter and the Internet.

Since the poems you find here were written specifically for this book, it is fitting that the cover image was also specially commissioned—and it is fitting, too, that a work of visual art should accompany these poems given the *Metamorphoses* has been the inspiration for so many paintings and sculptures over many centuries. There are a number of explicitly ekphrastic poems in the anthology—responding to works by Brueghel, Titian, Rover Thomas Joolama and Damien Hirst—with many other poems sharing that sense of '[s]omething amazing' described in Auden's 1938 poem, 'Musée des Beaux Arts'.

The poems here speak of the ongoing power of myth; they are in a sense meta-myths—offering a critique on mythology and pondering its persistence from the perspective of our scientific age. They are perhaps *metapoems* into the bargain (though wearing that credential very lightly); the subject is often matched by a poetic 'turn'—the sonnet-seed at the heart of so much poetry over the years, which continues to be influential today.

In compiling the anthology it made sense to retain Ovid's original order of 15 books and to arrange the poems according to the book and/or character(s) they were responding to. We placed poems that related more generally to *Metamorphoses* as chapter markers. We hope you agree that such an organisation honours the original narrative structure while allowing space for some modern transformations of our own.

We would like to thank the International Poetry Studies Institute at the University of Canberra for support in publishing this book, and of course all the poets who have contributed. We enjoyed editing the book and hope you enjoy reading it every bit as much.

Nessa O'Mahony

Paul Munden

BOOK I

THREE TALES FROM OVID

Deucalion and Pyrrha

We were pious and were saved. The rocks we threw
Turned into flesh. The flood receded.
The virtues of piety we commend to you.
Purchase your dinghies here. They might be needed.

Europa and Cadmus

Europa is a lot of bull, they said
And left, closing the door behind them.
Best kill your dragons now and pull their teeth.
But dragons are rare and first you need to find them.

Narcissus

I am Narcissus. My followers are here.
They crowd behind me with their selfie-sticks,
Myself at the centre. Soon they disappear
To be replaced by others, the sad pricks.

George Szirtes

THE LAURELS

In the heating and the dampening
we are coming back to the Med.
Daphne's humidity, Apollo never felt.
She closed one eye to that side of the world.

It's true we can grow how you prefer: bell shape,
box shape, curves with light and slender tips.
We also grow on stalks with twisted crowns.
What a god wants, a god gets.

The laurels are baying, they may say,
toxic berries that only keep one seed.
But she says, *if ivy poison you, or oak define,*
make a boiled poultice of my leaves.
Get ready to recognise our laureates.
Learn to spell your names again in mine.

Siobhán Campbell

DEBUSSY 'SYRINX' L.129

Music begins in panic.
The phallic chase of a god
goat-legged and mortal;
the lust-right, the thrust
and swell of the bestial.
Out of such chaos, flight;

startled flight of the chaste
into osiers to evade
the hot pursuit. No beauty
here barked over, no
passion dwindled to echo,
but into woodwind;

a score of windblown starlings
roused by a flautist's
breathing over reeds
to fly the rigid staves:
a murmuration;
a rough god chastened.

David Butler

THE EYES OF ARGUS

Put in his custody, poor cow, Io knows
that from his monstrous gaze she cannot stray,
those eyes are on her everywhere she goes.

So it begins, a life she never chose
poor cow who was a girl until that day;
put in his custody, young Io knows

how privacy's the mist a rich god blows
around at will to shape the world his way,
those eyes are on her everywhere she goes.

All thoughts, all dreams, the slavered, ugly lows
her mouth makes of the words she tries to say
put in his custody, poor cow, Io knows

that shade won't cover her, or night, or clothes—
her strange new skin, still white, is his to flay
with those eyes, on her everywhere she goes.

They stud his doughy head like raisons, close
for sleep in pair-by-pair infernal relay—
put in his custody, poor cow, Io knows
those eyes are on her everywhere she goes.

Enda Coyle-Greene

DAPHNE'S CONVERSION

Now Cupid's leaden arrow leaves her cold—
unmoved by mortal man or deity—
still stalked by god Apollo (hit by gold),
she won't get rid of him that easily.
The race is on, the two are neck in neck,
he is so passionate about the naiad!
She spurns his love, turns him into a wreck,
instead of leaving, though, the kouros stays.
To Peneus her Dad she makes a plea:
the nymph begs him to intervene and so
he transforms her into a laurel tree
but still the sun god strives to be her beau.
To stay a maid like your sister Artemis,
I choose the bay, with its plants dioecious.

Note: Dioecious refers to a species which produces either only male or only female plants (from the Greek for *two households*).

Maeve O'Sullivan

AFTER RENE MAGRITTE, *RECOUVERTE*

My mother had two faces.
One was solid rings of ancient wood.
Laws and rules were cut
into its polished surface.

Once she had been dark haired
and luscious
but slowly solidified.
I know there had been passion.
My father let it slip out.

The other face, a windswept tree
in the rain, looked over one shoulder,
roots so deep into the ground,
they couldn't be dug up.

Pauline Plummer

IMAGINE

A cat in the box.

Hold that thought.

Now imagine a goddess
Rising naked
Out of chaos: she divides
Sea from land, pirouettes
Each whitecap,
Rides a randy serpent
Until they're both spent,
Drops her egg into
Its Father's tightening coils
Until, split shell flaking
All creation tumbles out.

Hold on to that as well.

Next imagine

sudden light where there was nothing not even emptiness imagine that
spasm echoing splashes coalescing as dust snags dust onto blizzards
of new born stone that collide re-coil spinning energy mass a magma
globe first day dawning comets volley down first water rising as rivers
quenching first bedrock falling rain sowing seas where single strands
plait the first double helix that uncoils

through millennia into organised
Form: remember that cat in the box?

Well now she's a mewling kitten
Who's also an ageing corpse.

Finally, in no more than seventeen
Syllables, distil the above three images
And express as a metaphor.

Kevin McCann

OVID'S FIRST HAIBUN

Before the hybrid Lexus of the Emperor's agent had reached the bend
in the country road I had set my laptop on the table by the cottage
window and my carved wooden horse by the laptop. They looked
over the letter Q. Should I need to describe it in translation to one of
the poets of the East where they see our alphabet as something raw
or ill-refined, something lifted from nature, from its basic shapes, I
would set out for Q an image of an old pond and the path of a frog's
leap into it before we hear the ripples. It is the grey heron's eye and
her beak that pierces the pond's meniscus and plucks up the frog. It
is the inland sea and the flight of the heron towards it, drawn by the
tides and the habits of the small fry. It is the wheel and the exhaust
of the Lexus on a peninsula road charged with mayblossom and on
the steering wheel the hand and wrist of the Emperor's agent tasked
with driving the poet here into exile and with telling him that the
book that obsesses the people here could either be the lexicon of its
unique geography or an atlas of its strange dialect. Neither poet nor
agent look up to see the heron fly above them. It is the thumb and
forefinger of the Emperor's Chief of Police as he passes the agent a
pen drive with a list of poets to be exiled and their offending lines,
and it is the ring on the Emperor's ringfinger, the ring he turns and
turns as he tries to remember lines from the poems the chief of Police
told him, the one about the family as cursed as the Emperor's own,
the Emperor of another empire who imprisoned and raped his wife's
sister and was fed his own son stewed by that son's mother, the family
that turned at the prayer of the women from the rooftops and the
forests into nightingale, swallow, hoopoe, and then the other poem,
the one about the old pond and the frog.

> still as she can be
> heron marks the mother shore
> looking for movement

Matt Kirkham

MY BODY STEPS INTO HISTORY, IMAGINE

Unless I grow green leaves
And scatter perfume and petals
I must remain myself,
Stuck in my body. Time

Scatters perfume, and stars
Cover the earth at midnight.
Stuck in a body, in time
I might become something.

Dawn recovers the earth,
Telling the same old story:
Everyone turns into something.
Can't someone else shoulder

This same-told history?
It's always the woman looking
Over her shoulder, some man
Chasing her past herself.

Looking back, she only
Slows herself down. The sun
Chases her past her present, into
Time she must outrun.

Slow down. Even a god
Can't chase what won't flee.
Tempus fugit. Don't run.
Turn here, put your foot down.

Time can't chase if I won't fly.
I can't become myself
Until I put my roots down,
Unless I grow green leaves.

Katharine Coles

AFTER OVID

I

We felt our skins a little rougher each week. Hills fell from where we camped; the young stream was girdled in picturesque green. Old Adam might have appeared, so nascent-seeming it was, so rough-and-ready. One week you commented on the new feeling in your fingers; a few days later I saw you standing stock still—you sensed earth's vibration in your feet. A month afterwards you were green light and shade running between trees. You paused and shifting tendrils gathered your arms. I begged you to return, though your roots were in the stream, your hair a cascade of white blossom. You re-named me, a creek meandering between boulders.

II

The sky is a palette knife's spatter, trees heavy as the scene at Golgotha, wind bruising the day in purple swathes. A man stands on a diving board above a canal but doesn't step forwards; children giggle in a gondola, unwrapping sweets. Your words are blackbirds perched on gutters; our pasts are strung like lines of washing over a square. An old woman exits an alley, pulling a scarf across her face; a ball bounces into water, floating with an inane doll's stare. What we know of one another is mythology: a man with horns, a woman becoming a laurel—*citaeque victa labore fugae*—Apollo watching the heavy transformation, injured by what he has changed; thoughts weighing like lead in her, golden prognostications outrunning his chase. As the wind whispers, the water knows.

Paul Hetherington

O DAPHNE DOWN

her hair turns to leaves, her arms to branches,
her feet, so swift a moment before, stick fast
in sluggish roots, a covering of foliage
spreads across her face. All that remains of her
is her shining beauty.
—*Metamorphoses*, Ovid. Trans. Ian Johnson

Some 7000 people have died at the hands of vigilantes
and state sanctioned death squads in the Philippines…
—*The Guardian*, 9 May 2017

Look—the guns are out, the gods are prowling.
To the trees, to the trees! her feet urge on,
not winged like theirs, nor heavy booted
but bare, heels bleeding worlds—but where
are the trees? Just shadows of trees here, old
trunks rooted on asphalt, branching into crowns

of wires, electric as the charge in the air.
She smells their circuit of intent, the cordite
in the friction between steel and trigger finger.
The gods are baying like dogs—or is this just
a nightmare like when she sings and a drunken
god barks her name with his brand of tenderness?

O Daphne, come down, Baby, make daddy happy!
But the bouncer throws him out before her final note,
higher than that disco ball turning, prisms falling
on the stranger gods making them less strange,
all she can hope for in her red ball gown and glitters.
She is Daphne Down in this joint for the lonelier

than lonely   she knows them too well, pleading
for maybe Billy or Ella, girl. She's Girl, Girlie,
Baby, Love, Cunt—she can tell culture, class, corner
of the world from the name they cry, croon, call out
to her from the shadows. She can tell the weight
of loneliness in the note of their agro—how heavy

is the quiet weeping only she can hear? Each note
a tear contained in her throat, each chasing the next
Billy, Ella, Aretha, Janis—she's Queen of the Blues
after all, O Daphne Down! And before her, the gods
listen to their own heartbeat running her down,
urging her to *Come down, Baby, make me happy,*

even in her dreams where she is always running.
After his pants flared into skirts, Damian running
from his father's rage. After the lipstick earrings
high heels, Damiana running from the sheathed
desire of the corner boys, their sniggered names,
those bladed names—but now Daphne Down,

a redhead singing gut-you songs—then this god,
watching her for a week, whispers an invitation,
rubs the tracks on her arm, *your designer constellation,*
Baby   but she slips away and his lips tighten.
So the guns come out, the gods go prowling.
He leads the pack: *Get that drag queen drug queen!*

So Daphne runs Damiana runs Damian runs
under the lampposts, once trunks of trees now wired
and charged tonight with all the notes she sang
since the day she was born. *Hey Sister,* they sing
as her feet sink into the asphalt her arms branch
into cables her hair sprout into a foliage of fire—

and she turns, turns in all her shining beauty
to meet the gods and burn them all to cinder.

Merlinda Bobis

THE EYES OF DISHONOUR

now you may tell…

They cluster around you, the nymphs—
their scream foreshadowing Actaeon's doom.
And you, impervious to his bad luck, *more savage*
than […] *fair,* wield your wrath.
That's what the poet says in perfect ordering of facts
recounting a stroll, accidental wandering off
the beaten track, chance encounter with fate.
But if you look into it well, you will
find his words biased by his sex.

Fifteen hundred years ahead, Titian
puts Ovid to task, eye and hand brush-
stroking a gaze erotically charged as you bathe
naked and stripped of your bow and quiver
of arrows, rise, skin tingling with cold
and shame, curls clinging to your temple,
the nape of your neck, back; breasts shining
in dim light, the mound of your womanhood
barely showing above ruffled waters.

All quotations in italics are from Ovid, *Metamorphoses* I-IV Translated by D.E. Hill.
Warminster, Wiltshire: Aris & Phillips, 1985.
The epigraph is from the line spoken by Diana to Actaeon: 'now you may tell that
you have seen me with my clothes removed…' In Book III 193-4.
The painting alluded to is Titian's *Diana and Actaeon,* which hangs in The National
Gallery, London.

Dominique Hecq

CHANGE OF USE

I

If Neptune be the marriage of Heaven
and Earth and McQuaid God's man

on the ground, then Neptune House is home
for his deep rooted sleight of hand, populating

the Earl of Clonmel, aka Copper Face Jacks,
Georgian hideaway at Temple Hill, with little

children born of women without men to bind
them in the bands of holy matrimony, at sea

in a world of illegitimacy saved by life-buoy
McQuaid. With his eye on the main chance

J.C. sends in the Sisters of Charity to usurp
M.J. Cruice's abode for fallen girls, creates

St. Patrick's Guild and Infant Hospital, prices
each child's head, surer odds than McGrath's

Irish Sweepstakes. Behind granite walls, tall
trees hide McQuaid's domestic export industry

in plain sight at seaside suburbia. Neighbours
twitch net curtains but appear not to ask why

people come 'n' go, by foot and Mercedes Benz
in and out of high closed gates at Temple Hill.

II

Below the Virgin Mary, Sr. in-Charge writes
make-believe stuff up on babies files. Mixes

lies in truth as if snow-globes shaken, ensures
truth-flakes will not rise as nuns keep Mum. *In*

Excelsis Deo over knowledge to rights of blind
alleys they create, like slow burning incendiary

devices. Easier trace origins of Moore St. *Outspans*
than birth Saturn and Ops whose offspring stare up

at Patrick Osborne's plasterwork from row
upon row of iron cots, as if chickens in coops.

Their little arms stretch out to touch a ceiling rose
two horses high, or hope for hands to lift them up

leaves a remoteness that stills their inner lives.
Instils distrust as Doctors-in-Charge inject trial

drugs into legs that have yet to walk. To advance
medicine, in-camera investigations will say later.

III

After months or years of basic care, picked up
when necessary, left out in rain to study the fall

of drops amongst apple blossoms gone pale, or
follow cloud movements to the death of sunshine.

Gravel is raked. Daffodils yellow. Cars pull up
amidst footsteps and talk across polished floors.

Parlour doors open. Well-to-do couples leave
donations with Sisters of Charity for infant-in-arms.

Ball-park, seventy to a hundred thousand punts, babies
bound for Amerikay, less Lady Laverys grease palms

if left in the Republic. McQuaid's handmaiden's file
no tax returns if sent to Tallahassee or Termofeckin.

Little people whose antecedents will battle nature
versus nurture till kingdom come for arrangements

made. Commended into hands who will fail to shake
true nature from souls that refuse to be given up.

Anne Fitzgerald

THE FIFTH AGE

subtracted from infinity   human time
weighs hardly a flicker
which is why such divisions have use
four ages   a story   one that measures

so came gold   silver and brass   then iron
each valuing less   and less valued
greed for power ramping up
to compensate for the loss
people invented power and more power
over the frost the wind the time the flowers

and so the age of iron   you could smell it
the heat-ripple above taxiing aircraft
as they turn up their aim
as power leans back into flight-surge
over an earth measured in fields   surveyed
over a sewage culture of farmed suburbs
utopias of defilement and explosion
huge jets drizzling benzene
into the fires of refineries

was it so wrong to divide up time
into a story set against the invisible   incalculable
one that allowed humans to figure in it?
out of sight of land the pitching ocean
floated in miniature waves between clouds
just as the gods saw it

O Man   your own hell of a world
and the gods against you!
power was Jove's possession   and a few others'
soon enough a murderous revenge
delivered its final count
only the worst would suffice but what was it?

Jove spoke
not with a voice   more like a hovering shape

'why should we care?'   he said   'leave that to them
after the drive of iron the ache of bewilderment
complications too many and too great
freezing the joints
there's a cure   but they'll never find it
will go on looking   will not give up
the ant-virus virus of an antidote
on and on to infinity   worse than death
as for stardom   glory   empire   fame
let them go and write their names on fog'

so the gods listened   crouched together   feet in the sea
hands filling with lava and eruptive dust

Jove spoke again   a divine afterthought

'or we could change people into trees
birds   flowers   a spider   a bush of myrrh
in place of thoughts the rustling of leaves   leaves
and song   letting bark cover them'

Paul Mills

BAY LAUREL

Of course I made way for her; I had no choice.
The gust of that girl's panic
                          like a rush of wind
entered deep in the stuff of my cells.
                                    His rage

too like withering sun-glare (he calls it desire)
came crowding in after it
                          into the space
I was. I was spacious
                    not empty. I was everything

that earth and weather made of me: the high
green halls, the slow
                        dark conversations
with the light, the inwardness
                              invaded by...

you call it meaning. I say noise. Trimmed,
pinched to taste, that's my husk
                              repossessed;
myself, evicted
                into nothing you can place.

(That smell...) It is always an exchange:
for every nymph become a tree
                              a tree-
soul comes to, walking,
                        struggling to pass

in the crowd, still with her old shade in her,
with her thirst for transpiration,

                                    sap
cooler than blood.
                        You catch her eye

by accident; it opens in you for a moment,
between you
                    and the moment: laurel
silence, the fruit of the tree
                                of unknowing;

you're lost to yourself, lost for words.

Philip Gross

APOLLO AND DAPHNE
BY ANTONIO DEL POLLAIUOLO 1432–1498

Antonio got it right.
He knew what was happening beyond the rhetoric,
painters often do, even if they refuse to give it words,
it's there in oil and tempura plain to read:
it's not love here, it's conquest.

There's no forgiving. Look: see how her toes
carry the thrusting force of those thigh muscles forward.
She's kicking out at his grabbing hands, at his legs
still trying to get between her own even as they harden
to bark and pith. She's refusing all his claims
of adoration, flinging herself through the thin gate
of prayer shouting *no. No.*

Now her running spirit is coming to oneness
with forest and air, she is a green fragment,
part of the whole continuum reaching from magma
to stars, wildness grown dense and holy
as light within her. Her face pale with contempt.

This Lord of Delphi, Claros and Tenedos, this
very Sun, he would pleat her fizzing hair,
hobble her in high heeled shoes. I don't think so.
He doesn't get it; offers an honoured future of pomp
and dusty roads, marching generals, victories of war
her leaves to be his badge, trophies on his arm.
He thinks she nods consent when she is shivering
at the power of his delusion and has gone beyond him
leaving only the dry scent of a story told tersely

on a website, or by moonlight in a refuge;
or time after time in the kitchen, by a friend.

Rose Flint

THE FLOOD

It starts with drops and spots, that grow,
within minutes, to a dreadful spectacular;

a deluge thrashing the land, toppling walls,
turning paths to formless things.

It uproots trees, drags dogs from alleys,
turns the world to spray and foam.

It heaves folk from their drenched dwellings,
their hands aching for the sliding horizon,

tongues thick with mud. They spit their petition
for this to not be real, not now. This is the stuff of myth.

Miles Salter

THING

There was nonbeing before being. Before
nonbeing, there was no firmament, no air.
Yet something breathed. But where? And from what core
came all this water stretching everywhere?
So dark that darkness hid inside the dark,
nothing to show the deep, everywhere sea,
no death, no immortality, no spark
of birth, and yet the thing breathed windlessly.
Maybe it's in us at the nucleus
and all our thoughts are molecules awhirl
about unknowing force. Maybe for men
this being is God. Or maybe not. The world
prays to this nullity, Amen, Amen
(as if a thing like that would care for us).

Tony Barnstone

THE HUNGER OF APOLLO

It's the end of our first day walking, in the south of the North
Island. In the days still ahead, we'll tramp to the head of a stream,

then descend along the banks of another, to a confluence
with the great river, The Whanganui; first river on earth

to enjoy the rights of a person. All the way down, the ruins
of a bungled scheme for soldier settlers make chastening

company: Redundant windbreaks, chimneys askew, chestnuts
planted in trust and front steps into fresh air. This track is

named for the bridge at its end, an impressive concrete arch
and span across a deep ravine—it's The Bridge To Nowhere—

promised for the passage of farm goods but built too late; it only
eased the settlers' leaving, not hopes of home in the Mangapurua

Valley. All this belongs to the days that follow, for now we
shed our packs and step across wetted stones to stand at

the middle of a stream and drink in dusk descending, and shadow,
as it blackens the forest and valley walls. You, returning to

these islands you were born on—a landmass untouched by people
longer than any other—who finds the living away is often

unbearable, break the silence in tones not your own.
You speak with a lament-laden tongue—*This land is a woman*

held captive, she endures beatings and the rape of many men.
Before I can turn and see if it's a water-born spirit who stands

beside me, downstream a trailing, tuneless whistle, threads
the chill above tumbling water. *A Blue Mountain Duck,*

so *rare* you exclaim, thrilled. And back in your body; I can hear
you're a man again. In luck, we spot the pair—who mate

for life—fluent riders of the swooping current at its deepest.
Later, over the flames of the fire, in the sky where the night

weeps, a light-filled nymph, Daphne, flees in terror from
Apollo's rabid eye. Spent and almost within his grip, she

cries out to the river gods and begs for refuge. In this land,
her limbs transfigure not a Laurel but make tall the trunk

and slender the fronds of a Silver Tree Fern. The flames burn
low and tree ferns inch in to our shrinking circle of fire-light.

In pre-dawn gloom, we set our baited lines where the water goes
slick before it falls. While you break off tea-tree boughs green

to smoke our catch, I study an eel pinioned by its tail and twitching.
You remark how sweet, how human, the face of this dying creature.

Steve Armstrong

CYCLE AWARENESS APP

I thought
there would be
metamorphosis
in it
for me
a pulse
to tap
a spiritual
practice
the guides
said instead
I was a pin
cushion
I was
scooped out
like a melon
lucky to be
in this land
where it can
be done
of course
now
implanted
I return again
cyborg-tapping
the glass
creaturely me
on either side

Kimberly Campanello

BOOK II

OCYRHOE

Ocyrhoe was the human daughter of a wise centaur. She was turned into a horse for telling her father his fate.

You'll never deny her, they said, at my birth—
the spit of her father. What they didn't say:
not cursed with your horns, hooves,
lusts, feuds, the frantic burrowing
of your blood back towards the beast.

I had some of your stubbornness in me—
mulish, my teachers said, hearing in my questions
the echo of a jennet's bray.
When you hit me and said it hurt you more,
I could never summon the duty to believe you.

But I knew you. I knew the patterns in your rage,
could plot them like a chess player;
anticipate each move you'd make
as disputes became job losses, final notices,
long nights alone with all your knowledge.

One morning I opened my mouth to speak,
heard my voice sing your truth with such perfect pitch
it was as if I'd swallowed the blackbird's tongue.
You cursed me for seeing you as you were—
a hobbled half-breed who couldn't forgive

his daughter's evolution. But this time
the pain was worse for you, seeing me gallop,
freed of the words that choked you,
my muscles marbled in sunlight,
my throat singing *horse* to all and no one.

Jessica Traynor

LOVE

... it is my body that you tear.
—The Heliades

Once a young man fell in love with a woman.
She fell in love with him as well and for a while they were happy in each other's company. When they were no longer happy together the woman said she wanted to leave him.
He gave her both his arms and asked her to keep them as a reminder of their love.
Soon he fell in love with an older woman of poise and wit.
She fell in love with him too, and even loved him for what he did not have.
Eventually they became unhappy and the woman said she wanted to leave him.
He gave her his feet and legs before she went, and he said to her that these would be a reminder of their love that is now dead.
As the years passed he continued to fall in love with surprising women, gradually giving away his ears, his heart, and finally his eyes.
After this he gave up hope of being in love ever again.
He understood sad tears to be the useless gift one gives to the dead.
Determined not to weep or grieve over what was lost, he breathed only in the name of love.
He had many health problems and needed a carer twenty-four hours a day.
Strangely enough on a rare excursion a woman of his own age who still had her fiery hair and laughter saw him and fell in love with him.
She told him she wanted to live with him for the rest of her life.
He said, I cannot love you because I do not have anything left to give.
The fiery woman loved him so much she gave him her own arms, legs, eyes, ears and heart. Her laughter was loud and strong in her throat.
Once this fiery woman had given him everything he had lost, he stood up and looked at her and did not recognise her.

Kevin Brophy

BOOK III

READING HOUR IN THE ST. LOUIS GIRLS LIBRARY

I knew Narcissus lived on at the crannog lake
within the grounds. Smitten by his own exquisite head,
line of jaw, a sublime bottom lip made to suck,
bite, or kiss, and lustrous eyes, he ignored the cries
of evening curlews from November's glinting reed-beds.
Here too was Leda, undone by the brazen swan,

Jupiter. He drifted around the crannog in disguise,
paddled ardently, all dipped head, quickened eye.
Subtle the shift, fingers at first bewitched by depth
of feather, until her thighs unlocked to the rip
of his cock, then clouds of confusion that hovered
in his wake as she crawled away. I lingered long

past reading hour, learning from divinities, their antics,
trite cruelties. Worst was meddling Cupid, shooting
gold tips to stir Apollo's lust for Daphne,
whom he struck with lead. Pursuer and pursued,
Apollo's groin-soak never found release: she, feeling
no desire—an eternal virgin—stayed resolute as oak.

Mary O'Donnell

37

ECHO, OVERHEARD AT AN OUTDOOR CONCERT

Even here, as dusk lifts a new sound
even here, her voice abounds.
Listen: how she follows each chord
with her own note, how she chimes
in reply to drum and keyboard.
Oh Echo, we know how you wept

for faithless Narcissus, how you knelt
alone on the forest floor,
pillowing a cheek in leaves and loam.
You felt yourself sink, Echo,
first hips, then elbows.
To ripples of quartz, your veins paled.

Slowly, your gaze shed its shame,
hardened, began to change.
What was once a chain of pale vertebrae
turned grey, and you became a boulder,
touched only by fern, slug and rain.
The forest falls. A town grows.

Houses are born, new voices come and go,
and still, we find you here, Echo.
Wind brings clutches of soil to stone
so that in clefts that once were hips,
hillocks of moss now grow soft.
Sparrows drop seed to spring bluebells

and snowdrops by what were once your feet.
We hear you, Echo. Here, by the tree,
your whisper sounds soft and clear,
for you are here, still, in stone.
We call 'Hello? hello?' and listen—
listen for the reply. *Low. Low.*

Doireann Ní Ghríofa

ALAS, ALAS

I stalked him on Facebook, fancied him no end
bored my friends with descriptions of his lissom limbs,
his windblown hair, his carnal lips. Oh I just loved the bones
of him. I waited and waited vying for his attention, to get him
to mention me. I was a chatterbox, his beauty
silenced me. The day of the meet, I swore I would let him speak,
be quiet, hope he wanted to shift me.

Narcissus arrived on time, barely glanced up from his phone,
his mates pointed to me, his full red lips curled, he spat,
She's fat. I ran, I hid, crept into the cave of my room,
his words echoing in my head. *Fat, Fat, Fat.*
I swore then not to eat again, not to touch another bite.
I would be slim, sexy, skin and bone, turn my heart to stone.
I followed him on twitter, read his thoughts.

Weight sloughed off me, I toyed with food, mother
fretted, I fobbed her off, woolly sweaters fudged my shape.
I viewed all his selfies, he posted dozens every day,
at home, at play, in the street, what he ate.
He was a hall of distorted mirrors, obsessed with himself,
it didn't stop me wanting him.
I would get *Thin, Thin, Thin.* Resolved to try again.

Waylaid him on the way to school, offered
a bunch of daffodils, I couldn't speak,
dropped my compact mirror at his feet.
He bent to pick it up and took a peek, a gaze,
a long look and without lifting his eyes
wandered into the street. Alas, alas.

Jean O'Brien

REFLECTION

after Narcissus and Unrequited Love.

You can't photoshop this face in the mirror
A line here, a mole there, a spot at the centre
Each glassy encounter
Is knife-sharp as a razor

On the eye. I was younger, so were you
The upstairs flat smelled of its being new
At night the view
Over the rooftops drew

Us to nightclub music and the yellow ascent
Of other windows; who paid the rent?
I was too content
Some say, innocent

I was no match for myself. The lie
We lived aged us. The how and why
Passed both of us by
On the stairs like a coffin. I ...

Fred Johnston

TY-REISHA, LIRI, NARCISO

si se non noverit

TAROTS BY TY-REISHA
the sign says
FUTURES FORETOLD. CASH IN ADVANCE ONLY
An arrow angles down
to a midwinter basement
corpse-cold, smelling
of burst pipes and grave-must

She lets me in, 6 foot 4
in her snakeskin heels
– OK. you got the money, miss…?
Call me liri

Her hand stretches out, too close
to my face
– Put it there liri.
 One bill at a time
 I don't see too good these days
her adam's apple bobs like a dirty joke

– You sure 'bout this?
 Ain't nobody ever happy
 with what I tell 'em
I'm ready
she grasps my wrists
digs her chipped nails at my pulse
It's about my boy

***

Narciso leans over, neck bending deep   like a pale stem, stock still,
staring into a small square pool   in his palm, hour by hour,
stroking its glass face. it buzzes softly   with moon's light, hums with
infinite schools of brash fish, ripples   that will not stop, that
carry to the lip of consequence.   He cradles it, gazes
as the thickening weeds   reach up for him, green arms dripping

I came to leave his food this morning
and he was just gone, his phone abandoned

I scrolled through. He'd been chatting
with some woman called Eko
on Tindr
There were A LOT of selfies

My poor boy

– You best pray that child never know hisself
 's'all I'm sayin'

All the years I have carried this
massing burden
today I know its full weight
I can drop it; take up
my cleansing wail

Beside the phone, the plate
with yesterday's leftovers;
sprouting from the heel of bread
a small, perfect flower
some kind of daffodil
dangling itself at the screen

Melinda Smith

FORGOTTEN TALE

...his body vanished..
They saw a flower of gold with white-brimmed petals
—Echo and Narcissus

I was a girl born to humble, hard-working parents in a village whose name you would not know. More than anything I liked to play outside in winter. Wearing woollen gloves I'd mould fallen snow. When the nearby lake froze, a lad from the village would hew blocks of ice, load them onto his cart, deposit them in my garden. I'd carve them into figures of trees, birds and squirrels, flowers on thin, twirled stems like blown glass. I'd chisel precise portraits of neighbours and friends. My mother and father—a seamstress and tailor—disapproved of this preoccupation. They needed my help in the workshop. With my sharp eye, I was deft at embroidering. They also worried I'd catch a nasty cold. But I loved to feel the chill on my cheeks and hear the crisp ring with each tap of the chisel. I loved to watch the ice assume form, almost come alive. Sometimes, late at night, I'd steal out of the house through my bedroom window, and sculpt by the glow of a tin lantern. When the moon's face was white and round, its light alone sufficed, and I cherished the figures under the chalky sheen. Approaching the vernal equinox was the saddest time of year. I recollect clearly one dawn. Before my parents rose, I checked on the statues: though gilded and made translucent by the sunshine, a white egret's head was dripping like a tap, becoming indistinct from its elegant neck, undulant as a silver cobra. Next to it, a portrait of the cobbler's son was losing his bluish-white cap. Like a coat slipping off a hanger, I fell down in a mess, and sobbed. A young member of the emperor's cavalry happened to be riding past. I recall the assuaging warmth of his words, 'Hello there, can I help you?' I looked up at his radiant eyes and innocent smile. I felt I'd known him for aeons, as the moon knows the sun though they travel separate paths. I needn't tell you that we fell in love. Nor, perhaps, that my parents didn't approve. He proposed that we elope and find a place to live in the northernmost region where my sculptures would endure. The thought of leaving my parents weighed on me, but I saw no other way. We planned to meet at midnight under the full moon beside the birch at the lake's eastern edge. I arrived in good time. He wasn't there. I searched the vicinity, returned to the birch and waited. Though wrapped in thick layers, I grew ever colder. I cried but no one heard. Silver cross-stitches of stars blurred, and came undone from the lake's black velvet. Like a woman suddenly old, I withdrew into myself. Just before dawn he found me rigid as marble, my face white, eyelids locked, lips mute and as though stained by blueberries. The sun climbed over the water; its surface shimmered like chainmail. The wide sky was oblivious, an unobscured blue. He embraced my corpse and didn't let go. Three tears that had frozen on my cheeks melted and dropped to the soil. When midnight returned he shared my fate. (This I was told when he joined me as a Shade, and that he'd been delayed by an imperial demand.) Each year flowers rise in this spot: a living memorial, their white petals my three fallen tears. You know them as 'snowdrops'. Beside them, springing a little later, the sun-chalices commonly called 'buttercups'. Some time ago Ovid wandered by. I whispered this tale to him but he forgot to write it down.

Luke Fischer

ME, MYSELF AND I

Here's the sequel:
Narcissus gets tired of being a flower,
bribes a passing God to turn him back into a boy,
sets sail for the future.
He buys a load of instruments, wholesale.
Hires a multitrack recording studio
and becomes a one-man band: Me Myself and I.

Why the surprise? Metamorphosis
isn't always a one-way street.
That snake-basher Tiresias
spent seven years as a woman,
change being as good as a holiday etc,
before coming back to himself.

Narc (he calls himself Narc these days, with a hard 'c')
is living in LA. He drinks expensive bottled water,
never pond, stays away from his own
reflection in shopfronts
and drugs that exaggerate a sense
of self-importance—an almost impossible ask
in this city of self-declared angels.

Though he can't quite make it yet
in the outside world (too many temptations
to relapse, too many groupies),
his online therapist is teaching him that humility
will come with empathy. That he should
consider others less fortunate than him.

For that reason his songs are not original,
but covers of golden oldies with an twist. His ode
to Pyramus and Thisbe: 'All in all, love's just an
extra brick in the wall', has been a big hit.

And his homage to Salmacis and Hermaphroditus:
'When I think about you I have to touch myself',
seems to have twanged a common nerve.

But it's his elegy for Phaethon: the re-worked
instrumental from *Chariots of the Gods*
that has everything: tension, pathos, drama, sorrow.

He's almost let go all the heavy baggage,
but Echo has proved a stubborn hanger-on.
She's taken up residence in the speakers,
as feedback, to remind him of the old days.

A tinny reverb of what he once was,
just centuries ago.

Up himself completely. A lost cause. A pretty boy

who couldn't figure out if his was a lone voice
in the wilderness (some pallid hangover mirroring
his own words back at him). Or if someone
out there might actually be listening.

Once that trip down memory's meadow
would have freaked him out completely.
Now it re-enforces just how far he's come.

Judy Johnson

NARCISSUS AND ECHO:

PSYCHOLOGY TODAY

Narcissism is hot.

          What

Narcissists are so powerfully appealing

    is this feeling?

because you feel blessed when,

     Destined,

even if momentarily,

   unwarily

the bright beam of their self-

     bared. Melt-

love turns and shines on you.

down to rue.

The narcissist's heart is closed,

    Bulldozed,

but he is often highly skilled

sighing, thrilled.

at getting all he wants

   Goal of the hunt

through lying, passive-aggression,

my flesh and

manipulation, and control,

      soul?

leaving his victim exhausted,

Lost it.

feeling she has no choice.

   O, voice.

Moira Egan

TEIRESIAS LOOKING AT
ALL THE BIG RAIN COMING FROM TOPSIDE
BY ROVER THOMAS JOOLAMA

She calls him Teiresias the visitor who arrives each Thursday every second week of the month. Escorted by a young boy he shuffles up to the painting. The boy unfolds the stool and disappears leaving him seated to reappear after an hour to walk him out of the hall. What do the blind like him see? She wonders. In the evening a few minutes before closing she re-enacts the scene; her eyes tightly shut; her face firmly focused; and her hands folded in her lap. Please she pleads; please show me what the blind man sees. Frustrated she imagines herself walking his walk: the sway of hips, feet apart, and shoulders straight: the walk of a man in a woman's body or that of a woman in a man's body. But nothing happens; the painting remains silent; the seeing unconsummated. And then out of nowhere she hears the oracle-like voice of the boy; her face feels the burst of moist air followed by thunder; her hands move to shut the ears and she imagines herself turning into a wet streak of pebbles stuck in the sinuous crevice of a gracious rock. The rain falls and falls as she waits for the water to take her away hobnobbing with clay and sand, twigs and bark, flowers and nuts, skin and feathers. The metamorphosis has begun that will turn her into a fossil tucked inside the lithified embrace of a luminous rock. But the blissful moment lasts only for a couple of minutes. Once her eyes are open the ears turn deaf and her body inert. At home watching a lorikeet perched on the water basin in her garden she allows herself to believe that the moment of magic in the gallery would happen again. The hesitant hope begets joy faint like the smile on the face of the visitor she calls Teiresias.

Subhash Jaireth

49

from ACTAEON

Some of my friends are dogs; I mean,
real dogs. The way they go after
women. I mean, as if women
were a thing. A category.
Women are a construct. True word.
Doesn't stop my friends from being
dogs. Or—maybe, change the animal.
Julian more or less keeps stables,
whispers about warmth, depth, private
quarters; individual grooming.
Low lights and blinkers on, of course;
half-doors; careful angles; scheduled
exercise time. The females know
others exist by whinnying
and scent; both easily dispersed.
Ricardo just lets them like him.
He's surprised by every tribute,
in the right in every dispute,
constantly surprised when they go
away, go cold, go clingy, not
hope but expect. He's surrounded
by an ever-changing harem
visible to all his friends; in-
visible to him. For he does
nothing. Doesn't stop them feeling.
You see, my friends are men and dogs.
It hurts to think I'd seem like that.

Chorus

How beautiful the limestone arch,
how beautiful the pool, white, warm,
how clean of human feet, the sun lines
expression into water, set
and pouring, how beautiful the
limestone, between bone and marble,
senseless of the city lying
hot and elsewhere. Here the trees latch
so many and so changeable
gates growing alive and giving
way and not giving away this
place, where lilac flowers, tiny
under grassblades, uncatalogued
cannot be likened to trumpets—
nothing's been instrumentalized
yet, not even to make music;
a myriad voices in the moss
or via myecelium
underground is still a figure
of the kind of speech that matters
not, here. I would say the goddess
seeks to come down; small pigs with tusks,
reptiles free of panic fear, buds
and lichens flourish equally.

Vahni Capildeo

BOOK IV

BRIDES OF THE ENLIGHTENED HEART

after Alcithoe and Her Sisters

As the moss stitch forms between the subtle clatter
of the knitting needles, Sister Alice mutters her rosary.
Knitting has long replaced her rosary beads,
and the Aran cardigan forming in her lap contains
the fifteen Mysteries layered over and over
through its various patterns: figure eights, crooked roads,
double diamonds, rosebuds, honeycombs, blackberries.
The blood of Christ is washed white in the wool
of numberless sheep, bled invisibly into hundreds
of scarves, cardigans, bobbled caps. But none stained
by her own many bleedings, poured out unseen
in her eighty-two years until the seasons of blood
could no longer flow. A dull pewter Christ, one never
with blood to bleed, hangs stolidly and immortally undying
from the wall-mounted crucifix. Eighteen Angelus bells
intone the number of the great serpent, vibrating through
the convent walls. Sister Alice mutters another Hail Mary,
hopelessly out of count, her dentures clicking in echo
to the needles. Dusk begins to filter night through the dusty
panes, and the cardigan hangs limp and green. The carpets
now are thick with piss-a-beds and thistle, and her knitting
is a leafy dock. The nun's habit is a shadow, and she is dust.
But her mind is a creature with plumeless wings.
Through a gap in the ruined roof she takes to the sky
and joins her sisters as they flock in the deepening vesper.
All Sisters of the Infinite Heart, the bats crowd the encroaching
feast, where midges rise up from the convent's meadow.
The souls of the unbaptised, and the souls of the nuns
who witnessed their births, are gathered for a blood

communion. The nun's meadow slopes upwards
to the convent, its doors padlocked these many years,
the glass in its windows dead and lightless.

John W. Sexton

AFTER INO

wave-clattered shingle
      on a scrap of beach
and a woman
      is clutching a child
and falling out
      of an infinite ocean
that collapses and whitens
      around her

              [observers record the child
          whose skull was acquainted with rocks]

and a discord
      of seagulls
is grazing this woman
      with their wingtips
and beasts are beginning
      to gather

              [observers are fixed to the spot
      petrified arms outstretched to the water]

and this woman is cursing
      the gods who might
have persuaded
      seas to be kind
and kingdoms to offer
      safe harbour

                              [observers tear at their hair
                    and lament the futility of gestures]

and this woman buries her child
          and looks for the tracks
produced by the weight
          of people before her
and she follows these people
          and abandons the gods

                                                    Paul Maddern

LEUCOTHOE

The sun has my mother's face. Pointed features ringed by a mane of light, she opens her lion's mouth to heat the seed of unease that grows in my belly. In a graveyard in Boston, you tell me you want to be buried; your body returned to the earth when you die. Every night since then I have laid you to rest; exorcised your touch from my skin; your hands from my hair. The sun reaches into the earth and unspoken words rise from the dirt, clustering like white, urn-shaped flowers across your headstone. My abdomen swells to triple its size; an enlarged space for my pullulating grief.

Cassandra Atherton

BUTTERFLY LOVERS

I

Born a girl.
By my father's word,
plate of ash untouched—

Needle and silk:
opaline peacocks,
burning phoenixes.

Last of nine.
My hunger grows
beyond these walls.

Scholar's robes.
Books and bedroll.
Inkblock and scroll.

Alone on the road that leads
to Hangzhou. The path
crests the hill and broadens.

II

My study of the birds
is incomplete. I've watched them
land, lay, feed, and preen.

The caged nightingale sings,
its throat hollow, then filling.
The sparrows fly so swift

I capture only their shadows.
Once, I found a dead crane
by the lake: its soft neck wrung.

I'd set my birds free.
No one can understand
the waking between dreams.

Mind of poetry,
breath of calligraphy,
sweep of painting.

III

Yes we swore to be brothers
with soil as incense on the bridge
over the river under the pavilion

There we swore to be as one
we wrote couplets and drank wine
tried to catch the glittering fish

in red ink and in the moonlight
we recited verses stroked words
into the earth which rain dissolved

IV

These ducks on the pond
cleave the water like knives.
Beneath: the desperate paddling.

How does the story unfold?
The woman is given to another.
Masks, marriage and a grave.

The deluge: stormwater swells
the corpses and they surface.
Blind maggots writhing.

The caterpillar consumes itself in order
to regenerate. It will hurt to unmake. Wait;
transmute. Your wings will graft into being.

The Butterfly Lovers is one of the four great legends of China, and is set in the Eastern Jin dynasty (265-420 AD). It refers to the love story between Liang Shanbo and Zhu Yingtai.

Zhu, the ninth child and only daughter of her family, was allowed to go to Hangzhou to study, dressed as a man. Liang, a fellow scholar, and Zhu were as close as brothers, and Zhu fell in love with Liang. Liang was unaware that Zhu was a woman, but when he eventually found out and realised he loved Zhu, she was already betrothed to another, Ma. Liang sickened and died. On her wedding day, Zhu passed Liang's grave and is said to have grieved so hard that the grave opened and she jumped in, ending her life.

A pair of butterflies then emerged from the grave and was said to be the souls of the two lovers, united at last in death. *The Butterfly Lovers* has been said to be the Chinese parallel of Shakespeare's *Romeo and Juliet*, which, of course, originated from the tale of Pyramus and Thisbe from Ovid's *Metamorphoses*.

Eileen Chong

60

from THE WRECK OF THE UNBELIEVABLE

Venice, 9.IV–3.XII.2017

'nunc quoque curaliis eadem natura remansit,
duritiam tacto capiant ut ab aere quodque
*vimen in aequore erat, fiat super aequora saxum.'**

'those are pearls that were his eyes'
        —Shakespeare/T.S. Eliot

I

Punta della Dogana

Poacher turned gamekeeper, Hirst-Cerberus,
has wormed his way into the customs house
as faux guardian of these waterways,
hauled—from the deep—Ovidian treasures
while filming the whole charade: Proteus
in coral-encrusted bronze; a tortoise
cast in silver and gold; a mutant mouse
on the limestone foot of a colossus;
and a woman whose cling-wrapped body has,
for a head, the compound loudspeaker eyes
of a gargantuan fly. She's speechless,
like me, struggling—as the back of her dress
is breached by arthropoid legs—to process
the conceit: *Somewhere between truth and lies*

II

Palazzo Grassi

lies the truth. Here the coral has its hold
on toy Transformers; Spielberg's puppet shark
is gunning for Andromeda, SeaWorld
the logo glimpsed on a sword as your laugh
twists to a loss adjuster's casual grin.

Then I see the snakes of Medusa's hair,
carved out of malachite, and imagine
how labourers, doing his dirty work—
chipping poisonous dust into the air—
hoped their contributory craft might morph

into genuine art. His sketches bear
an anagram signature: *in this dream* ...
I'm telling all this as if I was there,
and perhaps I was. What have I become?

* Even now corals have the same nature, hardening at a touch of air,
and what was alive, under the water, above water is turned to stone.
                                                                —Book IV

Paul Munden

BOOK V

CALLIOPE'S SONG

If my song is broken
it is because I sing of rupture

I sing the abduction
of the child picking flowers
her tears for the scattered violets
her screams for her mother

I sing the mother calling
the mother vanished into her loss
I sing the mother who finds her child
I sing the mother who will never find her child

I sing the woman
who changes to repel
the violence
before the violence changes

I sing the woman as pool of tears
the woman forced to change
the woman who transforms herself

I sing of her
who risks herself to protect another
I sing of her who bears witness

I voice the woman who will never speak
I voice the silent call to the crisis line
I sing of her who speaks and is not heard
I sing of her who is heard

I sing as a woman together with women
for the woman alone
I sing for the survivors
for those who are gone

I sing because it is by singing
I tell stories
that must be told

I sing for those who will never sing again
I sing for those who may not sing
I sing for those who believe they will not sing
I sing for those who may sing again in time

I sing for those whose song is not broken
I sing for those who will sing again
even if their song
is broken

Catherine Ann Cullen

ON WAKING

There are no gods.

I do not seek you out in some twisted underworld
of mist and shadow where deities go undisputed.

I walk on cold ground.

Myth brings such little comfort to the powerless.
I draw on a cigarette, back pressed to pebbledash.

It flickers, sputters smoke.

She had her day. Married in silk, in late summer;
high neck, sheer overcoat. Plucked the memory

for more than twenty years. She had the marriage,
mortgage, home. Birthed three wriggling children;

two healthy girls survived.

Still, she was glad of him; the three years of a tiny
hand in hers, never begrudged her daughters' smiles.

Love was not enough to save either one. Cut off
five days past forty-five is much too young, too much

to bear. I confess I tried.

They said this country had been rid of snakes, choked
up on the venom I would have sucked from her chest.

They lied. I did descend

into a certain kind of dark and found her in a slumberworld,
alive, tight-lipped, nonchalant on the periphery. Daylight -

you are gone all over again.

Stephanie Conn

SCYLLA

The night you, handheld, limbsplayed, served up
the sweet shallows to the salt of my lips

as the bath bled heat we were near the edge

of empires, a gull's wingbreak from Atlantis.
Uncrowned, you and I, returned to water, fleeing rain

and the terror of flags. Always you wanted to be barely

touched, lepidopterous, called on, not pinned. A thirst
sipped risking hunger, wrinkled skin, discovery. Come

dawn the ache of sleep gnaws like blind fish at the brink

of our heed. Road before us, no names to leave behind
for the chaste clouds to stumble over trying to call us back.

Alvin Pang

NEWT

The Rape of Proserpina

The idea was to shrink him down a
size, that bold-faced little turd who
laughed at Ceres' pain, her daughter
gone missing, seduced by Pluto,
vandal of the underworld.

Down it was: here they drift through
waterweed, sculling, laid back, four-
toed freckled salamanders hoiked
out with gushing reeds when I was
cleaning with the garden rake.

They bypass the scrum of sex to
reproduce; there's decorum in the male's
meek offering of sperm, the way she
takes it to her cloaca, glues eggs
safe to the waterside of leaves.

Soon tadpoles flicker below surface
tension's silver skin; gills stream H^2O,
tails elongate, legs sprout for landfall, but
winter will pass before they venture
back to seek their kin.

I had to laugh at him in my hot
palm: bewildered, bereft, blinking
as I put him down to slither back
to water's cooling silks. Sleek
adolescent, half-grown eft,

neither one thing nor another yet;
juvenile delinquent taking to the deep,
cocky with the awkward gait of some
thing not yet grown, his instinct
anticipating winter's sleep or

peering up through water's wobbly
lens, all previousness a far-off dream:
Ceres searching for her violated child
in white-burning rage that plunged
her howling to Pluto's realm.

He was a bit-player in that quest,
collateral damage of her losing race.
But still, there's happenstance in fate—
comeuppance made him wizard
of air and water's interface.

Graham Mort

BLOOD ORANGES

Let me remember blood oranges,
a windfall just on the brink,

the sultry afternoon we tore open
their rose-fleshed segments.

Each mouthful remembers
a sting of zest, a glut of cells.

What did we know, still dazed
from the fall. We'd gone

too far into the charmed garden,
loving oblivion for its stealth.

The afternoon light was
the texture of dry tinder

with all the touch flares
of a volatile sky.

You must remember how young
we were, the blood sweet surfeit

still warm in our bellies.
When a clawed shadow

observed our trespass,
you wept. So it goes—

thunder harrowed heaven
split the future from itself.

Lust and treachery, the gods' mirth.
Let me remember the blood oranges.

Peggie Gallagher

CYANE

moon pool, colour code for blue
Cyane is older than us all
river home for a Sicilian nymph

but she was no nymphette
she stood up to the death god
abducting her friend Proserpine

called out to him *stop, this is no way*
to gain a wife let her go   Pluto
in self-rapture ruptured earth

Cyane stood in silence, wept
and wept yet more, with each
new tear her body dissolved into fluid

her hair blue as the sea melted
limb by limb shoulder by arm
she wasted away in grief for her friend

when Ceres arrived all speech
had been swallowed into liquid
no words just bubbling and burbling

but she showed to Ceres the sash
of Proserpine and Ceres knew
the truth of her daughter's abduction

in Syracuse they remember Cyane
her transformation her metamorphosis
from young girl to sacred blue river

Inspired by Book V, Translated by Brookes More: "But now the mournful Cyane
began to grieve, because from her against her fountain-rights the goddess had been
torn. The deepening wound still rankled in her breast, and she dissolved in many
tears, and wasted in those waves which lately were submissive to her rule. So you
could see her members waste away: her bones begin to bend; her nails get soft; her
azure hair, her fingers, legs and feet, and every slender part melt in the pool: so
brief the time in which her tender limbs were changed to flowing waves; and after
them her back and shoulders, and her sides and breasts dissolved and vanished into
rivulets: and while she changed, the water slowly filled her faulty veins instead of
living blood—and nothing that a hand could hold remained."

Susan Hawthorne

74

BOOK VI

ARACHNE'S METAMORPHOSIS

I was ready to wring my own neck,
to avoid the injustice of a rigged contest.
It was my own fault, I was the challenger,
puffed like a cobra: sure of my gift.
I should have minded my own beeswax:
I, a mortal, rearing on a god.

She wasn't born humble:
she burst out of Jove's head
after he'd gobbled her mother.
She wove herself into the centre
of daddy's charmed circle, sewed hard
to show their awe at her victory
in winning the city. She garnished her canvas
with punishments, meted out to those
who refused to knuckle down.

I have to laugh at her so-called wisdom,
her precious olive branch.
What I got was a box in the head,
when she laid her eyes on my brilliant conjuring
of Jove, and his shape-changing rapist pals,
busy with their brutal deflowering,
disguised as eagle, bull or swan.
Furious with envy, reeking with poison,
she tore it from my loom,
but, clinging to the moral high ground
she forced me from my noose—
my freedom—distorting my limbs,
so she could boast of mercy; of reprieve,
declare herself mistress of the situation.

Left to crawl in the shadow of leaves,
I lurk in a silk net pumped from my gut.
But, as I abseil from great heights,
spin on my whim—each day a new pattern—
my vision of her curse transmogriphies.
These days she's just a statue: solemn,
helmet stuck on—no spindle, or flashing needle
—even her shield, carved with Medusa's gorgon grimace,
hangs quite still.

My daughters run wild:
many-limbed and eyed, by the time they're born,
their fathers have already been devoured.
Swift weavers all, expert in the hunt,
survivors with their wiles, and much admired.
Mother of such girls, I rarely hanker
for the old tapestries—
frayed and faded in the sun of many days.
Dawn offers fresh vistas in the garden:
intricate circlets, shining with dew,
more satisfying than any crown.
As Minerva languishes—eroded; barren—
with nothing for company but her brittle owls,
I declare the contest finished—I've moved on.

Katie Donovan

FOX NEWS

Was it the sung line *a mighty fine town-o*
That set me at odds with the country cousin
Who sat up nights with the loaded shotgun
And claimed his bounty of fifteen bob
Proofed on the bloody tongue?

Half a century of little ones' little ones
Now urban themselves, stark in the moonlight
They stop to establish the terms of the treaty
Before vanishing into the hedge.

Until the morning after the builders
Had skimmed the newly concreted driveway
I woke to the Hollywood dainty paw prints;
The knife in my hand, raw words on my lips:
"Nothing to say for yourself?"

Iggy McGovern

WEAVE

Minerva called it a curse,
      to sit at my loom

morning to evening
      as long as I live,

winding the warp,
      rolling the weft,

threading the heddles,
      throwing the shuttle

back and forth
      through the shed.

Now I'm old as the earth,
      I call it a gift—

I've learned that a weave,
      plain, twill or satin,

can't be made
      without the loom's rattle

and lanolin oil
      for sore fingers, stiff limbs.

Jane Clarke

SUSPENDED SENTENCE

SPIDER, convicted wordsmith, permanent spinner of narrative,
(intricate comedy, intimate tragedy, infinite history)
I was committed for life meaning life to relentlessly jabbering,
loomed on a loop is my telling, the middle, the end, the beginning...
SPIDER, a.k.a. Arachne, queen of the alphabet,
challenged Minerva to mix it up on the mic, my mentor,
goddess of wisdom and war and schools and commerce and art,
she represented the gods and I was the voice of the people,
twenty-four hours our lyrical tournament-parliament-argument,
arrogant she, but more arrogant I got a standing ovation,
jealous, she judged and she juried me deep in the slough of despondency
then she pretended to spare me by making me SPIDER; I ask, is it
better to die for your art or to live in perpetual servitude?
let me hyperbole, show how I flowed in my past participle:
oh, how she tore up the airwaves and oh, how I virtual tapestried,
weaving my left-winged words on the www,
ordered the QWERTYUIOP into quotations and quatrains,
questioned the status quo in freeflow stanzas and stories of
gods who were dogs, frogs who were snogged, hogs who blogged
newspaper articles trolling the truth in Times New Roman
and so many shades of blue that the greens and the reds got the Blues;
then Minerva, goddess who chinkled Chateau Margaux with the gods,
counterattacked on the web, how she heirloomed, how she airbrushed
crimes against humankind but goddess was kissing thin air;
in the final War of Words, the last Battle of Bards,
I, with my full-throttle, flexi-lipped lexicon, murdered the microphone:
'Square Mile Midases sinking their teeth into gold-leafed burgers,
six-digit salaries flicking the V's at the minimum wages
metamorph the mint to a stiff-little-fisted austerity,
verily, even the velvet and ermine who pray to the one

true God (with a capital G) are occupied by divisions;
gods of the ABC transpose the curriculum vitae,
cutting and pasting the 'c' and 'creative' morphs to 'reactive',
adjectives, articles, predicates, crushed into neat little boxes;
inch-high headlines libel people who risk their lives on
rickety boats in nauseous seas with nothing to eat but
prayers into 'immigrants', 'aliens', 'criminals', 'predators', 'cockroaches';
gods disagree, should this island remain with Europa or leave?
Exit disguises itself as a man and seduces Brittania,
Brexit is born, a three-headed beast that feasts on fear—
foraging, fattening, threatening ...' people, I would have said more, I'd
barely got into my narrative flow but mentor went mental:
spammed my memory, poison-penned my Achilles heel,
turned my brain to a bare-knuckle fist till words were anathema,
meaning was meaningless; beat, deleted, defeated, I placed my
neck in the 12-point noose of my glistening narrative thread
and she, Minerva, seeing my muse surrendered, suspended,
acknowledged my criminal skill on the mic, and delivered my sentence...

Patience Agbabi

LEDA

we didn't have a choice in the matter
the matter was they needed the land
the land that cannot belong to us
to us it was home but they made us an offer
an offer we couldn't turn down from the gods
the gods are all in government here
and the government here wanted Liede Village
Liede Village was promised highrise apartments
highrise apartments and a communal park
a communal park with a running track and lake
a lake with ducks and swans for the village
so the village upped and moved, like a game
like the games that were coming to the city
the city that prepared its flags and banners
its flags and banners were waved in the village
but the village still doesn't have new apartments
new apartments or a park or a lake of swans
of swans that had no choice in the matter.

David Tait

GUSTAVE MOREAU INVITES

'Leda' at 14, Rue de la Rochefoucauld, Paris.

Moreau's mythos finds
in a fairground of light
desires we cannot fully see.

Temptations of flesh
that cilice cannot spare.

Spirits emerge between walls
and the cracks of doors.

They gain their levity
searching for gravity.

Hummingbirds stuffed in a bell jar
slighted into meaning, bending the bough.

The family tree frowns
at Leda, who undresses.

The Hydra frightens and the Sphinx
scratches to blood with her claws.

Nerys Williams

PHILOMELA OF HOMS

My first soft body broken open when they smash
through our front door, trash me and the house.
Pain and shame cut out my tongue, until

my changeling feet in dusty sandals split and curl,
nails into claws, bones thin to thistle-down,
shoulder blades itch and twitch,

flesh splits again, searing. This time bursting feathers,
bloody wet, opening, arcing. Wings rise above my head,
the lift of flight, skimming over the rubble of my home.

At dawn and dusk, song surges in my throat like bile,
my frozen voice grown so much larger than my body,
thawing, insisting that one day I'll be heard.

I set out mapless, trackless, as ice-winds
fire-winds lift the feathers on my back,
onto a journey the wild geese might dread

not knowing which strange branches might cradle
my chicks, under which cold stars, towards a place
where I barely hope to find welcome or rest.

Philomela was raped by Tereus, who then cut out her tongue. The gods turned
her into a migratory nightingale.

Maggie Butt

MARSYAS

We think Marsyas is the only one
who changed, stepping from the forest
to challenge Apollo, staring at the god

he could never rival as if
into a harshly lit mirror, each recoiling

at what he found there: the jealousy knifed
inside the mortal talent, the cold perfection
threaded through with rage.

But then the muses stirred behind them.
And Marsyas, out the painful human wish
to be admired, cannot help but play.

And afterwards, the cutting,
the stripped corpuscles, the ruined mouth--

                  Only after his victory would Apollo reach out
and clip three small muscles from the satyr's throat
and shoulders, and dry them on a rock, and string them between
the curved horns of his lyre. Then the god

would pull a song
through that tender sinew, telling himself

it was not the crying of one
who's lost everything he loves but the god's
own singing that he heard, and after which
the muses strained, because it was the song

of someone who knew what it was like
to be alive, which the god could not bear
to know, or to stop playing.

And so Apollo, unthinking, binds himself
to Marsyas: the god taking from his rival

fear and desire, the satyr hardened by the god's
cruel skill, until both songs

writhe inside each other, sung
by one who cannot understand death, and so

never understands what he plays,
knowing only how his hand
trembles over the plucked muscle:

adding, he thinks, something lower to the notes,
something sweeter, and infinitely strange.

Paisley Rekdal

BOOK VII

MEDEA SYNDROME

On the muted TV news
a red Fiesta swings below a crane.
Water spews from yawning doors,
we glimpse a booster seat, transformer toy.
Yellow tape rails off a stone pier
where locals pray, a cop props wreaths
and teddy bears against stacked lobster pots,
the rescue team stows gear.

The barman turns up the sound...
suspected murder-suicide.
Kept to herself, a neighbour says, *devoted to her kids.*
Over crisps and pints, the regulars wonder
what went through her mind
when she floored the pedal.

And a punter at the bar coins 'Medea Syndrome',
says when he took up with the new woman,
Jason's foreign wife stabbed their sons
in spite, then steered her red Fiesta
headlong for the sun.

We turn away, watch evening drawing down,
the ferry out at sea.

In her homeland, they tell a different story,
that Jason's cruelty pushed Medea
to a mercy-killing.
Some name their daughters in her honour.

Breda Wall Ryan

FOREST OCEAN

Who grew in fields ten times the village ground
within a narrow clearing? A small tribe, whose
forebears had spent whole lives pushing back
the wood's edges. Being forest folk, whose gods
were trees, they paid careful homage, sprinkling
blood and water on roots exposed before the cut.

Trunks, split and planed, made walls and floors;
branches, straightened, trimmed and bound,
made roofs; the rest prepared for slow burning.
God-smoke in the slow evening, floating away
from here and whispering through a living canopy,
where tides of air not water swept through days.

Of all the children, that girl, Dercea, and that boy,
Arteus, were sweetest to behold and did the most
honour to their village, with green eyes cast down
in thought, cast up eager for teaching. This being
a time of plenty, a wise mother was allowed to take
all those who wished into the grove of learning.

Where daylight paused to breathe, she took three
maps, silk-woven in strong colours, folded tight,
and laid them on the ground for telling. Each one,
unfolded, would be two man lengths wide and long,
a view from high above of land-bound lives they may
have known in their labouring and dream-full sleep.

In the clearing, while others watched, with her arms
reaching full-wide, she gripped the silk and cast it
open at the feet of gathered pupils, young and old.
The first map with so many varied shades of green—
a world they knew but far beyond where they might
track the way from their own clearing to any other.

They saw what might be other villages, like theirs,
cut into the forest, each with its hive and the glow
of honeycomb beneath the foliage. The whole world
open at their feet made the real forest around them
more intense, so all the birds and insects they knew
began to sing at the same time, carrying them away.

Arteus gleamed, his eyes knew Dercea, on the circle's
far side, but he saw her indifference, no light showing
in her eyes, no joy taken in what she saw. The others,
animated at first, grew pliant—entranced by new trails
among familiar trees. They did not see a second map
arrive, another wide-armed stretch as a world landed.

The endless forest greens contained within a peninsula,
narrow, sand-bound, surrounded by soft and dark blues
of sea, swollen and swaying with strangers' promises.
Arteus followed Dercea, saw her leap and writhe in air,
entering the stream and leaving a momentary rainbow
where he flew with wings, not arms, wavering through.

Wine-light sea glimmers, her strong-scaled flank dives.
Leaf-dark nights he sleeps in the hive, his sweet labour.

Oliver Comins

BOOK VIII

THE CONVERTIBLE

Evenings they'd cruise these streets in moult,
windows wound down, each radio thumping out
its carnal beat, high-fives on reds before the fuel-injected
jolt, the foot-down, flat-out roar of engines

and the whoops of crew-necked gods. They'd wave
and toot their horns at him as he stood watching
from the high windows of this house I'd paid for
from a life-time at El Sol, the factory my own father'd built

that I still drove to every day, dawn till dusk, in the fin-tailed
gold convertible gleaming in our driveway. She was
heaven-sent, one of a kind, a Phaethon De Luxe V8
automatic, her white tyres shining steeds hoofing

the ground. He shone too, this son of mine, and he *was*
mine, no matter what some folk said about my ex,
and when he turned his blond curls towards me I looked away,
afraid of what was coming. 'If you really loved me

you would let me.' Anything but this, I begged him,
knowing she'd be too much for him; knowing that he'd never
rein her in. But he'd his heart set; how could I refuse?
His grin as she erupted at the slightest touch of pedal;

when he eased her out the gate he waved back once
before he gave her holly, scorching off into the distance,
heading west. Ahead the highway, the hot tar's
shimmering meniscus, and the quivering, open mouth

of the earnest young policeman
later on the doorstep, his hands twisting the cap
he's respectfully removed, the night behind lit up
by the squad car's pulsing blues. 'Bad bend',

he said, his words becoming torn metal, the pylon
buckling on impact, jags of lightning hissing
from the writhing cables, and the river churning
where they'd found his catapulted body

in the ravine far below. O my beautiful, my broken son!
Now he rises once again, borne skywards by the helicopter's
dripping slings, over the stricken poplars and the silent chorus
gathered on the roadside, as if this machine hovering above us

could reel in all of this, could unwind time to a time
before the dying fall of light: the sun-struck streets,
still empty, waiting for the songs of cars; and a boy
dreaming of oil and chrome. As if we could go back.

John O'Donnell

I WANT TO BE LOVED LIKE SOMEBODY'S BELOVED DOG IN AMERICA,

those you see let run, let cavort on golf courses,
their ears flapping—Papillons, breed painted
by the masters, gazing up
like cherubs at their overstuffed mistresses
in the lounging days of other lost

empires. Bounding past flags, they orbit
the solitary figure they possess, swirl
the green knoll, not led or managed, tethered
or commanded. I know they are
fed by hand on a lap as they age; palms up

the moist offerings arrive. They pick
and choose, leaving something behind
to indicate they are aware of bounty, of the bounty
bestowed upon them, the love with its lap,
with its pamper and cloy, the voice above them

at a height like a wooden flute riffling the universe—to
soothe, to mollify a beloved glance among
the comets and dying suns. Theirs not to be
held like coyote or slow-eyed wolf
at the rim of the fire-circle, but

invited in, tempted by the half-picked
carcass, delivered from the snarl and tear,
from approach and withdraw. Still, wildness
confuses my tameness. If I scorn,
you supplicate. If I cower, you assume

my past was of the usual brutal sort that leaves
my like—abandoned. If so, let me
be abandoned in America, then sucked up
by the greed of guilt. Pull down from the high shelf
the one thousandth variety of '*Bison Mixed with*

Chickpeas'. Oh America, allow me one day
of your righteous distain
of poverty. I have a longing, a passion
to belong to something heedless and full
of mock-conscience. I might design a few

domestic habits to let it seem
I'm adjusting. You wanted a slave, a heel-licker,
and to enter the house first
with masterful stride. But I changed
all that with your beneficent rescue

of me—my pleading gaze,
as if worship came naturally to me, whereas
it plunders me, scrapes and hollows me out. What
had I hoped for in this intimate duet
to which I proffer only the arsenal of teeth

and primitive memories of a hunger
that knows how to tear
life out by the throat? And I gave that up,
for you? Caress me, my Lilliputian centaur.
I have a much-delayed appointment

with adoration, with the mercy
of your half-baked causes. Let me scratch out my
little-American-dog-will, leaving you
my rhinestone collar that used to casually strike
stars of blood against the back of your hand,

my dog tags with *your* chosen name for me, remnants
of my perpetually uncertain battleground, phone numbers
etched on them in case I should lose you, a water bowl, a
coat of fleece. Oh America, you looked after me

so well, with your chokehold-lead and your
Microchip-identity—proof of ownership
riding my neck-fat. I never had to swim for it
from a sinking boat. The heated bed banished
the roadside ditch, banished distain,

and when I lay down near your feet
it seemed I had chosen my lot. Yet what ambition
can this level of satiety allow? The swift narcotic
of the moment tenders more than you
suspect. A small Ultimate, born out

of my loyalty, gradually arises to provoke you
to gaze past fountains and glass palisades. You
who know how to squander, put down your
pretense at wholesomeness. I am lowly
and raise you up, but to a purpose, as with all

who are helpless before might—to become
that something that thinks *in* you,
whose trusting regard works a change on you
from inside where you never intended
to shelter me—the one who attends

in order to interrogate, to unravel
the inoculation of your pitiful kindness-agenda.
Consider the world and its poor, its suffering—
you see how it is when something speechless
begins to think *into* you, to manifest, to bear down

on you as our double-self dissolves?
Shall we cower and beg together now? Forgive
the kick and the cage? I'm feeling tender
toward the largesse of this undertaking. 'Come, Toto,'
I hear, like a last endearment before sleep. But

by then the living-differently of sleep's velvet lining
coffins the whole of it—my plundered
ever-after heart, your incremental
changes—as those onlookers think you someone
once worthy of me—that little nothing-Titanic
of your sinking days.

Tess Gallagher

BAUCIS AND PHILEMON

Oh my gods but that was some feast—eggs still warm from the coop,
more clutches than we had hens,
purple plums saved from the blackbirds' beaks,
sweet and plump as babies' kisses,
clods of our goat's cheese in milky cloths, a honeycomb's golden ooze,
the last of the meadowsweet mead that never ran out.

Villagers called us crusties, hippies, blow-ins; we lived by the old ways,
rose with the sun, honoured the moon, kept bees to complete the circle.
I'm not saying we weren't worried when two gods came calling,
in disguise, as gods do to amuse each other.
They showed up, footsore and gnarly, hounded from the other houses;
in our valley, we saw few strangers.

We received them warmly, for who are we to turn away another,
bid them freshen up then spread out my best hemp blankets.
What little we had, we shared; we opened our store,
fetched peppery radishes, pink as rubies, pitchers of clear mountain
    water,
Baucis's vein-roped hands cradled figs and autumn nuts,
a willow basket of crabby apples, cornelian cherries soaked in wine.

They left replete. We asked no boon, needed for nothing,
hale we were and hale we stayed;
perhaps we just forgot to die.
But one small favour they granted first;
Baucis wanted never to see my grave
and I requested never to bury him.

On the last day before pain and loneliness,
our bees swarmed in the glade; their thrilling buzz filled our ears.
We leaned together, grew leaves from our limbs, bark coating our skin.
The last thing I saw were my love's sweet eyes smiling at me.
We turned to oak and lime; roots joined, in the way of trees,
we continued our lifelong conversation.

Kate Dempsey

ERISYCHTHON'S DAUGHTER, MESTRA, AT AL-ANON

As I never thought to ask
how you had been cursed
with such insatiable hunger,

it was out of love I sold myself -
at first. Young enough to think
I could shape-shift destiny

I returned home to discover
you were still masticating
the domestic detail of our lives.

When I slipped my bondage, remade
myself for each subsequent sale,
cold anger began to gnaw at me.

In the end it was Neptune, took me
by the hand. I turned away
as you turned on yourself, ravenous.

I carry that with me, but horizon
too is mine—I open my eyes
to find, beyond circumstance, sea.

Nell Regan

FALLEN

And when the wax melted and she slammed into the water, she remembered all those who tried before her: who'd leapt from mountains, cliffs, towers and columns; those whose belief in the impossible was secure, those of us who have longed to soar with birds, ride thermals with ease and know how to catch the earth's slipstreams.

She watched cirrus clouds touched with gold as the sun sank beneath the Mediterranean waves. Felt her blood darken like lost hope, pooling at the back of her skull. She thought of her father. He was one of life's dreamers, one of Larkin's *lecturers, lispers, losels, loblolly-men*.

Overhead, a murmuration of starlings swooped and curved across the sky. They were mocking her. A jumble of feathers, broken tibia and fibula.

Her father's daughter. Her fingers burnt.

Anne Caldwell

WHOM THE GODS LOVE ARE GODS THEMSELVES

[Disguised as mortals] the two gods went to a thousand homes... and found a
thousand homes bolted and barred against them
—Baucis and Philemon

When they set out in hacked-out boats,
great holes in the panels instead of controls,
no way of directing destinies—who knows
whether there are gods hidden among so many?

If there are no divine hands, no tillers to steady;
if they survive to make desperate requests,
these strangers pleading to be our guests—
which household will let them in? It stirs

Phrygia's scorching summers, freezing winters
into our harsher climate
of exploitation and profit.
But if someone hurries

to bring them wine-soaked cherries,
plums, fragrant apples, grapes just-gathered,
or even to replace their tattered
T-shirts and jackets, give bottles of water—

perhaps the old gods will draw closer
and change such capacity for kindness
to unbounded hospitality and a timeless
wish to be transformed.

Robyn Bolam

BOY, PIROUETTING

Observe this feather falling
   through the draughtless air:

      the plumb line of its spine
        is wrapped in a spinning whorl

      obeying muscle memory
     that's neither flesh nor bone

  and steered by downy barbs
like neurons too small to see.

Still, its stillness turns,
   unspooling its own surprise:

      evidence of gravity,
       not bound by it.

Anthony Wilson

THE KITCHEN CHAIR

This is an old chair. Built by the first hands
to gather the wild seeds and make them tame.

For years it belonged to Priapus, God of vegetable gardens,
worshipped by the people of Lamsakos in Asia Minor.

Not just a chair, it is also what you might call a *grace*:
For what we are about to receive, make us truly thankful.

Some things have been forgotten, for somewhere
in the journey from loam to market stall, from green-grocer
to supermarket to hypermarket, from agriculture

to agri-business, we lost touch with the nature
of growing things. With the great age of the wild white carrot
that was already old when the dinosaurs roamed.

With the value of radishes—the coin paid
to labourers who built the pyramids in Egypt.

With the medicinal properties of lime—
preventer of scurvy, and once a military secret
that kept sailors safe at sea for months on end.

Time was we knew the worth of growing things.
Sweet potato, ginger, pineapple, each has a story
of lands and people we may never know.

I dare you to sit on this chair.
It will give you the eyes of a gardener,

will gift you the days of sun and rain
wrapped within the layers of an onion,

will let you hear the chime of the slow clock
that ticks within the word *harvest*.

They say one tree can produce four hundred apples,
meanwhile its leaves put the breath in your lungs.

Sit here and you sit in the lap of the Earth Goddess.
She has placed her cornucopia in your hands:

asparagus, aubergine, apple. Banana, carrot, courgette.
Melon, lettuce, garlic. Strawberry, rhubarb, fig.

Formerly kings did not live so well.

Grace Wells

THE ACORN AND THE HUNGRY KING

He, in sleep, in imagination, dreams of feasts, closes his mouth on vacancy, grinds tooth on tooth, exercises his gluttony on insubstantial food, and, instead of a banquet, fruitlessly eats the empty air. *

The voice inside the oak sings a high tannic note,
bitter and herbaceous like squashing a sodden

teabag on your tongue until your throat contracts
in revulsion. Those who say its song rounds out

a good sherry, ignore repressed memories of blood
inside the wood, the trauma of the swung axe blade

in Ceres' coppery grove where the Dryads once held
their ancient sacred dances, writhing under votive

tablets and garland wreaths. Bite into an acorn,
and you can taste the faint sweat of those nymphs,

before the aftertaste curdles your stomach with fire.
Desire, the Buddhists advise, *taṇhā,* that Pali word,

remains unquenchable, bottomless, a belly ravaged
by famine, like the curse that befell old Erysichthon,

the Thessalian king, when he felled the massive oak,
then fell himself, first ear-sick, then heart-sick,

then forever ravenous, munching the air to breathe,
swallowing whole olives, pit and all, sucking honey

from the bees' hives and milk from the very udders
of his royal cows. The more he devoured, the more

he had to devour, but it was like pitching drachmas
into the Aegean, if the coins were wholly immaterial

and the ocean infinite. He drained each amphora,
only to grow thirstier. He ate until he had his fill,

and he never had his fill. Finally, he began to gnaw
on himself, beginning with his digits, then his hands,

then his very arms up to the elbow and beyond,
crunching bones and sinew. Isn't that the meaning

of craving? The nature of addiction? The hunger
sunk deep inside of you that tries and tries and tries

and tries, but can't get no satisfaction? The dead man,
as a living man, devours a dead man, himself, still

alive, but slowly, surely, dying in excruciating agony.
That's us burning coal and hacking down rainforests.

That's us at the turn of the millennium. Think of him
next time you order a particularly oaky chardonnay.

*Book VIII:777-842 (translated by A.S. Kline)

Ravi Shankar

BRUEGHEL

In 'The Fall of Icarus',
a creation parable
speaks to us:

the ploughshare folds
over the arable
earth, to match the folds

of the ploughman's coat.
We also note
the fold, the divide

of the horse's tail.
The painting's insides.
its intestinal tract.

Attention to detail.
The unimportance of subject.
Subject as pretext.

The bent legs
of the anti-hero
are there only to echo

the configuration of sails.
And to be part of a chord:
ploughman, horse, shepherd.

Their chorus of legs,
of dance steps,
executing a gigue.

So here is Toby Merrill
of Russell and Chapple
stretching a canvas,

lost in the process.
The picture is face-down
on a piece of polythene.

The frame in bits,
a bundle of sticks.
He uses a rubber hammer to fix

slats into slots. The fit
has got to be tight.
The dimensions have to be right.

Hear the tinkle
of tape measure
across the angle,

a calibrated curvature
corner to corner. Whoops:
the metal's sudden droops,

its refracted erections.
The staple gun
awaits the stretcher:

a four-inch-wide pair
of sturdy steel pliers
like a laundry press

for starched collars.
They grip the canvas,
bend it to its will,

hold it still
to bang the staples in.
What follows

is the same routine again.
Removing the staples,
one by one,

and re-stretching,
tightening the hessian,
until it is taut as an apple.

The final wooden wedges,
with tapering edges,
tapped into the corners.

And each corner holds
its origami, its intricate folds.
Which brings us back to Brueghel,

to Brueghel and this girl
putting her child to the breast,
for an hour, her eyes at rest,

absent, inward, unaware,
with concentrated lips,
her factual hair

held by four hair grips.
She might be taking a piss,
or doing her business.

Craig Raine

DAEDALUS AT MIDLIFE

A light rain has come
                    in the night like sleep—a better
Sleep, a softer fall, a kinder kind of waking

Than I have known in years. My body lies and longs
For rest my mind won't let me keep. A grief two decades

Deep is all I know each dawn. I lie and implore
Sleep to hold a while yet and steep me whole

Again, and, when it won't, and won't again, I cry:
I'm done with life. With living on, if sad is all,

Or most of all, a man can be. If anguish—gone
Last night—is going to break each day, then give me death,

At least for now, until this agony has spent
Itself upon itself—and laid waste time—and passed:

I'll come back then.
                    I rise instead into a clearing
Sky and as the light unspools like thread and spreads,

And wrens reprise again their 'Blue in Green', the rain
Begins again. It falls as sound, a peaceful piece,

A steady riff, my mind—unmanned by this too much
To bear, and lost in work my heart should rather do—

Would like my coming days to learn. I'm called, I know,
To fashion a life, without the tools I used to use

To shape one. Somewhere here I have them; I set them down,
When life and work—which until then had seemed so much

Like play, and earth the envy of heaven—fell down and drowned
The only child I used to be, and orphaned me,

His father.
                    If only the dark would throw some light and help me,
Blind, to find them. But this is an old man's plaint;

I'm exiled from myself. And through my craft I've made
Of all that's left of life a labyrinth I'm lost in.

Under the hands of the masseur today—who divined in my back,
Bent too long at the work of my mind, reservoirs

Of sorrow deep as seas and older yet than tides—
I began to drop into the body of my grief.

The world is made of metamorphoses: each day
Becomes the next. And I'd become myself again,

If there were gods who'd hear a prayer these days and nod.
But no, it wouldn't be the life I had, my mind

Too bright with wings that flew too high and far. This ageing
Life, this father self, is all that I'd become.

To grow my mind some legs and walk it back into
The way things are: the brokenness, the rain that falls.

'Blue in Green': jazz piece by Bill Evans and Miles Davis. I have in mind the recording by Bill Evans, solo piano, 1960

'Peaceful Piece': 'Peace Piece', improvised by Bill Evans and first recorded in 1958. 'unmanned by this too much/to bear' references Robert Frost's 'Directive': *back out of all this now too much for us.*

Mark Tredinnick

SCYLLA: A SEQUEL

By mid-February 1947 the mercury
hadn't risen above zero, my father said,

and four swans, a sister and brothers
who'd been here forever, took refuge

to the leeward of Limerick Point
for a lunar month (as cut off

as the small town itself in high snow drifts
between Lurig mountain and the sea).

They were joined, that little band, he said,
by a way-off-course heron, harried all the way,

or so the story went, from a far-off Mediterranean
by a pecking white-tailed sea-eagle

that was, in truth, her father, Nisus,
eternally furious at a beloved daughter's trickery.

Bird-headed, they conversed, on those frosted
sub-zero nights—with only strings of ice-bound

Greek or Romanian trawlers lighting the distance
between slipway and Moyle horizon.
                                    Much talk

of perilous straits, of well-foundered ships
on wine-dark seas. And of Scylla's alter-ego,

the monster, spied, over centuries, in the deep loch
of the great Highlands glen to the north-east.

(Seems the banished Black-Sea-shores poet wove
one Scylla into another.)
                        Until they realised

—that Hellenic heron, those Celtic swans—
that writers always use banishment, alas,

as the cruellest penance for betraying
your father, your village, your country.

(Or berating an emperor, like exiled Ovid
in Tomis.) Or for driving vindictive stepmothers

like Aoife to metamorphic fury.
                            The swan siblings
had flown by the time I was born, mutated, perhaps,

by chapel bells into the aged kind of people
I watched shuffle to daily mass.
                           The other Scylla,

that six-headed wrecker of ships
with the sea-monster body and tail hasn't been

sighted for years now, just as we never saw
such biting winters again.
                           But the heron,

more peaceable on finding sanctuary, maybe,
on wintering out with our enduring
swans,

still has her roost on Limerick Point, and her rightful
place in my own first five books of exile.

Anne-Marie Fyfe

THE LITERAL

after Jack Beckstrom

The literal is a curse in bronze skin, with strange hands
polishing breasts and belly. It's an unseasonably cold morning
in a city without myth, a city that makes up new legends daily,
and only the occasional tourist notices the statue rising from tulips
as they rush to Instagram the next landmark. But hands convey life
to ivory, to marble, to bronze; thumbs pulse sensation, humanity
deeper than art and advertising—and I wonder what questions
she frames first beneath her hair's stiff waves? *Where are my friends
in this imagined century? Who left me naked in this merciless town?*

I can't stop to ask, as I've library books to return. But later I see her
on an open-top bus in the rain, shivering in a souvenir sweatshirt,
but smiling beatifically. *If you look to your right, you will see
an empty space in wind-blown tulips—a sculptor and his apprentice
lost for words.*

Oz Hardwick

BOOK IX

ALCMENE'S DREAM

after L205-326

I dreamt I had a son:
a chubby, dimpled child
whose blurry eyes shut
as he fixed on my breast
and sucked my life from me.

I gave it gladly. Nobody spoke
of the spite that midwifed me,
the servant love that freed.

Men told of twelve labours;
what did they know of seven days,
of seven nights pushing a hero,
cell by cell, out into history?

I woke to a dusty corner
where a cradle might have stood.

Nessa O'Mahony

BOOK X

EURYDICE AWAKE

I kept
my visor down, waiting
like a courier in the lobby
for someone to come. No one came,
there were no instructions, no
guides or plans, no signals
crackling in the headset.
Where were you? But then
it came to me, the wreckage
spilled out all over the hillside,
the mitigating, falsifying acres
as if the whole country had killed you
or none of it, or nothing claimed it—
threads of a tunic, bloodstained clods,
hair and nails, a broken plectrum,
the body parts, the mutilations
when they showed,
like videos calmly posted ...
It was all
forensics and after-quiet
and I gathered what I could
crouched in the dusk
singing softly to the hillside
and carried the bag back down.
No one looked or queried. The transports
were full and everyone tuned
to their own devices.
I sit now in the lounge
reading the report and playing back
the old music and you come

prancing through the headphones,
swinging the mike from hand to hand
as if it was all still waiting,
the stadium full and the lighters flaring,
everything plugged in, tested,
ready to explode,
and I had stood behind you, arms stretched out,
your body retreating to my breath,
your shirt falling on my eyes
as you yell redemption
and strike the opening chord.

Peter Sirr

GRAVE MUSIC

According to the Tibetan Book
of the Dead, although a body
will not come alive again once
the heart has ceased to beat,
for forty-nine days the corpse still hears,
each day more faintly, until our
voices can no longer reach it.

But what if that body, although
dead to us, and mourned, slips
from one realm of sound
into another? What if a
different music filters in,
earthier, its volume slowly
rising as the coffin lowers

inch by inch into the ground?
What if Orpheus' music were playing
still, trapped in the strata of
the underworld, between silt and sand,
mingled in the soil we walk on?
Or plays itself through roots,
worm tunnels, tendrils

fingering the dark, faint
murmurings, soft susurrus
trickling through the dank
conglomerate of clay?
And what if our own music,
made and played by human hands

and hearts, were nothing but
a quest, a search for harmonies
from another space and time?
The fiddler at the graveside,
the jazz sextet, the marching band—
all echoes, subtly caught, of airs
we sometimes think we hear
on starry nights.

Geraldine Mitchell

ORPHEUS

Still in the Iron age, the singer Orpheus travelled
through iron screens hiding his lean body and lyre in
the luggage compartments of vessels, trains and vehicles.
He passed borders, entered the underworld and returned -
curled back into himself, shocked by what he saw ahead.

Still in the Iron age the fish had metallic aftertaste
and barbed wired fences bordered those who believed in walls
to keep them safe—while they famished for love. But Orpheus called up
the trees who were once lovers of gods—now transmuted.
He wrought his grief into a heavy metal song and made
the furies cry for a whole season. Famous inhabitants
of the underworld stopped in their routine robotic work,
now gazed into nothingness, reminded of something hard to
grasp, forgotten but seated deep in the soul. His talent now
discovered through the ex-factors the gods took pity and gave
Orpheus a passport that said he was homeless but free to go.

Still in the Iron age the gods in full knowledge of power
decreed: 'You can sing for us Orpheus but never look back.
Sing us the songs of lovers we want to hear, you and your kind
have a chance in "the fair play". In our times of globalised
pleasure it is hard to know where is under or above, but
the compass will show. Follow the metal to civilisation—
you only need Gold to live well in the underworld.'

Still in the iron age Orpheus cared too much—and looked back.
Sentenced to live a long life as a Bacchanalian—
Singing the twisted stories of passion—lovers adored

and betrayed by the gods, only released by transformation,
singing sorrow songs of lovers, the famine songs for love.
He moved forests, birds and beasts, melted hearts harder than rocks,
till one day—deaf to his singing voice—all the women he once
rejected in his home rose against him, stoned him to death.
Speared with iron, his body torn to pieces, his last breath
on the wind, his singing head still wobbled on the white river
enthralling the waves to swell with tears, the trees to drop their leaves—
he was freed to go to the Elysian fields to meet love.

Csilla Toldy

RETURN

Like a cat who brought home his kill,
laying it out on the hall floor,
a dead blackbird, chewed and torn—

the bride he stole from the meadow
was robbed by a master
with a hunger for blood.

Each tale he spun was of war,
threat, murder; his mind, a tomb
full of lost limbs, bodies found,

drowned infants. Summoned,
a ghost, to greet Orpheus again,
with only the weeds on her skin,

and since by music was led,
she dragged her ailing foot
up the ascending path, that mute

dark track. And reaching upper air
she trained her eyes on his neck,
inhaled the living breath,

breeze off the lake on her face.
Heard voices of children at play.
Music drift from the square.

Dreamed her wedding bed.
Quickened her step.
Saw his turning head.

Catherine Phil MacCarthy

ORPHEUS AND THE TRAJECTORY OF LOVE AND FAME

Change, my agent said, *sing*
something new and different.
Your gods of love and loss are so
same old, same old.

My audience was shrinking, he implied
-the fickle swing of the Zeitgeist. What
do I care? Eurydice still leads me, though today
our dance cannot be merry.

Those high notes I once uttered
came straight from her lips. It was
a dual entrancement, charming
pale Naiads into song.

Be like me, she said, close and mysterious
and my voice rose higher
in vocal arabesques that almost equalled
her rainbow feet.

Love stories inevitably go sour,
my agent says. A veteran
of three divorces, he sighs world-weary
over the sheaf of morning hopefuls.

Yet he recognises the quiver
of talent. Innocent beauty
still sends his hand to the phone
to wheedle new deals.

She'd never have stayed with you,
he tells me, meaning his words
as comfort. *She was one
of those free spirits no one could hold.*

I followed her though auditions, tours, shows
then into the underworld of clinics
through the groves of desolation.
Believe in me, she whispered.

But for an instant I faltered, stepped
outside to tune my instrument,
though my heart was breaking,
I thought to spur her to recovery.

A bird called and I looked back
through her window. The shades of Hades
gathered her up while my error keeps me
chained to unrequitedness.

Máiríde Woods

THE SLIP

In the Underworld,
I drink up the sleep
of a thousand deaths,
forever dying, yet
never free of you.

An ever-death, towards
endless shuffling;
elongated end,
a replaying of
dumb morality.

Shock me into
a consciousness,
eternal dream
of some release.

Might you come and
moisten my dreams
with a broadsword
of your music.

THE TURN

The faith that is firm
is also patient,
knows to wait inside
the cyclone's cold eye
before passing by.

Even tornadoes
can hold calm centres,
such serenity
against the violence
lashing out, turning.

Those who travel
ahead of winds
can grow to fault
their company,

presence mislaid,
compass points lost
when North is the
only concern.

A conscience
returning,
too sacred.

Night-time,
always.

Look.

For down here,
there is no
harmony.

I'm close,
closing.

Onwards, on
we must work
the road up.

A pace
too far.

Gone.

Familiar,
my old hand
is waiting.

A head
in doubt.

Colin Dardis

MYRRHA

Having fled the bed of her father,
game all the family can play
but a crime nonetheless
and not without its warnings,

from her own conscience to the horror
of her nursemaid who turned complicit
or the owls unearthly screeching
when night was missing her fires.

Nine months of the wanderings of shame,
exhausted, she halted in the perfumed
place of Saba, hardly able to carry
the weight of her womb.

Pleading to the heavens
that she didn't want life on earth
or by passing below, death.
'Refuse me these, change my form.'

As she spoke, the very earth crept
over her feet, roots sprung from under
her cracked toe nails, bones became wood
and her marrow flowed with sap.

Arms thus to branches and fingers to twigs,
her alabaster skin gnarled and bunched
to form bark. The tree soon encompassed
her pregnant belly and pendulous breasts

growing toward her neck. She plunged
her head in the trunk of encroaching bark.
Myrrha's emotions were lost with her body
but she continues to weep honoured tears.

Resin distilled from the bark carries her name.

Joseph Woods

THE OTHER MYRRHA

Her newborn boy was fine, considering, but afterwards she wouldn't
look at him or hold him. You've heard of that thousand-yard stare?
The baby was so cute we midwives nicknamed him Adonis.

Her confidential file has all the backstory. The kid's name was Myrrha,
her dad, Cinyras, a donor to every good cause and the ruling party,
her mother, Cenchreis, a youthful beauty. As their darling fairy
grew into a pouting teen, with a lovely little figure for her age,
her mum got jittery, criticised Myrrha's clothes and mentioned *jailbait*—
but her dad would offer drinks and tell her friends what men preferred,
poke fun at spotty boys, say teenage girls were *so much more mature.*

Myrrha had a secret to torment her, twisting the bedsheets as she lay alone,
pondering her father's view that these things should be learned at home—
look how, in many cultures, girls were taught such private arts by older men
who knew what they were doing, not their clumsy peers—surely his
princess
was worthy of no man more than her daddy who knew what was best.
In the animal kingdom, billy-goats and bulls would have their way
with any available female, including their own offspring, and sire young.
It felt good, didn't it? So how could it be wrong?

She practised her own pleasure, conjuring Cinyras' words, his hands,
his eyes on her, until it came to cutting lines on her limbs,
a little minor blood-letting, therapeutic as far as it went, and that
is how the housekeeper caught her out, while her bewildered mother
was away on a pilgrimage with the ladies of the parish. This temp
her father hired was used to sourcing girls, and knew he liked them
fresh—men will be men—so soothed and sweet-talked Myrrha,
led the youngster to her parents' dim-lit bedroom, where one side

of the king-size bed was vacant, and Cinyras had chilled champagne.
He refilled the teenager's glass 'til she was giddy, murmured *baby*,
pretended not to know whose voice replied. And to tell the truth,
he did know what to do—unhappy joy! After a week of this, her tongue
tasted of metal, the first sign that she would be a mother to her brother.

On the ninth night Cinyras heard his wife come home from her devotions
and let herself in. The lights came on. He shouted, *Myrrha!*
What are you doing? Get out of my bed, you slut! and lashed out fast
to silence her, but Myrrha dodged his fists, sprinted away, hitched to the city,
ate at soup kitchens, walked lighted streets by night, slept in doorways by day,
evaded do-gooders, concealed the bump—afraid to live, afraid to die.

At home they whispered, *What a little madam! Cinyras and Cenchreis*
reared a cuckoo. Of course he didn't know! He was asleep, tired-out,
poor breadwinner. They spoilt her rotten. Next she'll appear in some enquiry,
accusing her own father, the drugged-up hussy! Cenchreis doubled her visits
to the House of Prayer. The clergy were especially sympathetic.

And that's how Myrrha came to us at St Lucina's, numb and speechless,
wooden-faced from shock. The baby went into care, the girl to a hostel,
leaking milk at first, then silent tears—institutionalised, an icon,
a moving statue—wiping the communal kitchen, mopping the floors.

Gráinne Tobin

PYGMALION

for Joseph Walsh

And in the end it is this that I return to—
thing of my own making that loops upwards

like branches thirsty for light, reaching high
to the glazed roof where the river gulls balance

close to the city's slate-grey sky. Listen now;
how they scratch and squawk their racket of desire

but they will never rest or nest in my carved olive ash,
rooted in limestone below in the long courtyard where

four vast windows have opened again to light that floods
the walls of white ceramic tiles, floods my graceful looping

art that I go back to in the end, ascending with it—
oh, my perfect imperfection—rising to sun, rising to shadow

all life there in its smooth wood that night beckons me to touch.
Then it is woman, her skin beneath my thumb soft as wax in heat

and I gather marigolds for her, burn incense at her tiny feet, sing
sweeter than Orpheus ever did, press a ring upon her every finger

and in the early hours, leave feverish for nightfall again—
our love renewing itself, assured as tomorrow's wedding bells.

Enda Wyley

AN APPLE TREE FOR RUBY

You can run as fast as Atalanta
who bowled three apples at her suitors
Double Red Delicious

with skin that blushes, almost empurpled
incarnadine on the grass
causing them to bend and stumble

and with strong white teeth bite into
flesh so juicy their chins glisten
as they raise their eyes to catch your heels.

Elizabeth Smither

OF THE MYRRH TREE *COMMIPHORA*

Opopanax, balsam,
bdellium, guggul, bisabol—
scented resins of myrrh,
the pitiful tears of Myrrha
who fled from Cinyras,
from the bridebed of her father.

Over nine moons of waning,
she awakened in a village in Arabia,
their child Adonis swelling,
a stone in the apricot of her,
that sapling of her lust
planted in her by her father.

By adulterous Cinyras.
No god uproots his future.
Stained Myrrha, daughter, praying.
One god conjures his answer.
Which is to bring the women elders
of the village with their razors

to slam her down, splayed,
to sever her of pleasure;
to abandon the girl, bleeding,
in the grace of that god's favour
in the grave-grove of his Sahara
in answer to her poor prayer.

That god's pity is a cess of leaves
spilling over Myrrha's shoulders;
his pity is her toes tearing roots
into the midden beneath her;
his pity is her slight limbs straitening
into her fingerprints' growth rings;

his pity is needles of lignin
eviscerating her viscera;
his pity is the auxin of shame
stealing across her synapses,
the photosynthesis of breath
making her every word vapour.

Silence at the heartwood of her heart.
Silence of the leaves of her palms,
the drip-tips of her fingertips.
Silence of her arteries furring with phloem,
of this sapwood of her skin,
of her death-mask of lichen.

And as the slow bark's sprawl
swallowed Myrrha, closing
over her hair, that god,
her father, whispered:
Beloved Myrrha. Daughter.
I did this. For your honour.

David Morley

A NOCTURNE FOR EURYDICE

For '*the maiden in her dark, pale meadow.*'

Twilight through the roof of a rainforest
      shatters like a chandelier of green glass,
the shrillness strafed by keening cicadas
      and unseen flocks of cockatoos that caw
their catcalls at the meltdown of the sun.

Dimming of the day bronzes a pathway
      that we follow under vaults of booyong
down a terraced stairway to this canyon
      of warm mist, where a waterfall loiters,
draped in a grotto, like a soaked sarong.

Shadows deepen the tinges of each fern
      to jade, while we descend into the nave
of this cavern where paramours gather,
      unmournful, by the cascade to witness
the arrival of bright nymphs at nightfall.

Prattle, muttered by the gentle shower
      in its pool of shade, softens our voices
while we wait, rebuking the ruby glow
      from a camera, its lamplight forbidden,
a red ray doused to darken the drama.

Lovers who kiss near the railing confess
      their joy upon seeing the mossy shine
of dew, luminescent on the black walls
      of rock, these blurry photos of bijoux,
mimicking shimmers on radium clocks.

Umbral, the day-glo from every fey fly
　　　　stipples the cave, pinpricking crevices
with a spray as numinous as absinthe,
　　　　the basalt hung with threads of saliva,
like dewdrops bedewing a spiderweb.

Wonder spins a tinsel that embroiders
　　　　our mood as we marvel at this roomful
of miniscule creatures, each flea as far
　　　　from us as a star, whose constellations
loom over us, guiding us to our doom.

Glyphs, unreadable by the wispy gleam
　　　　of foxfire, foretell no fortunes for souls
who appear with their private oracles
　　　　to view these tapestries, then file by us,
like a queue of lanterns leaving a mine.

Bereft of our path when left in the dark,
　　　　we take delight that, blind at the entry
to this shrine, we find a dim dot of red
　　　　taking flight, a matchhead lit in a waft
of perfume, its spark lifted like a kite.

Adrift, the speck is our distant galleon
　　　　with sails ablaze at night upon a black
ocean, a feeble beacon whose glimmer
　　　　disputes the puniness of living things
that strain to remain afloat in the void.

Clouds of pollen, orbiting the orchids,
        ignite, then cavort, alongside the banks
of the cataract, each downslope aglow
        with muddled smudges from luciferin
in green fungi, blemishes of limelight.

Unease amid this awe that consoles us
        still impels me to grope for a guardrail,
retaking your hand in mine to guide us,
        like a blindman, up a cliffside staircase,
unseeing in the blackness what awaits.

Lovers know that, of all demons in hell,
        love is the most dire, dutybound to tear
all spirits to tatters, to spare no thought
        for the remnants of misspent romances,
which defy the gods but end in despair.

Deeper than this ravine with its river
        flows a duller stream of forgetfulness,
our dream, like some oasis from chaos,
        where devils avow that, if love is woe,
best then to dwell alone in the cosmos.

Regret is the ember that calls the moth
        to burn in the spittle of a glow-worm.
Let me keep my faith aloft, like a flame,
        my firm gaze, unreturning to this rift
behind us at the blindspot of my loss.

        Let me promise bravely to uphold you,
though we falter at the threshold when we cross....

Christian Bök

#STICKSANDSTONES @HOUSEOFRUMOUR.COM

#makeyourselvesathome #rumourforall
#talkaboutphilomela #echo #midaswife #aura
Nightingales deserve what they get, the bitches.
Yeah, so true. **If she's so pure**
she wouldn't be a nightingale, right?
Define pure #wrongendofstick
I fucking hate nightingales.
I've been a nightingale and I know, it's not the whole story.

Guess you believe Io too, cow-lover.
Sticks and stones #wounded #fairerworld
All gods are rapists.
Who are you calling rapists?
I know where you live and I will send thunderbolts.
Bring it on.
She wrote in the sand #Io
OMG with her hoof. **Tears streaming down my face.**
Lame.

She loved a flower.
Nobody loves a flower.
I know where you live.
Where you live?
Show me the evidence.
#evidence lol
It was down by the pond.
#pond

Stone her with words.
Mud sticks #mud #river #assesears
Down by the river guess what she was.
The reeds heard her.
Sticks and stones too good for her.

He killed her because he thought she was a beast.
Too right, they all beasts, the bitches.
What is your problem?
She misheard him.
That's what she says.
Two sides to every story.
He killed her because he was a rapist.
He's not a god.
It's not just gods are rapists.
No, it's you too. You rape with words.
#givemestrength #houseofrumourrocks #philomela

Amina Alyal

THIS IS AN AETIOLOGICAL STORY

after Cyparissus

I loved a boy
a fine stag haunches
thick as root
antlers garlanded
in the sun

Took him under my wing
let him pluck the feathers there.
When my finger ran down his trunk
it felt as though a pause ...

He would lie and I
watched him sleep
until unthinking
I pierced him.

I beg, let me mourn.
Let me weep
as a tree weeps.
Let me sleep in sugars

and oils and cells
hardening my fingers
forming against the sky
an outer bark dead

head aglow pointing.

Shane Strange

BOOK XI

SINCE WHEN THERE HAS BEEN MUCH WATER
UNDER BRIDGES, MUCH WEEPING

The Silk Road so blurred provenance
that Linnaeus was convinced

(Or was it with an eye to Heaven?)
by the imagery of Psalm 137

in his naming of *Salix babylonica*.
It was in fact *Populus euphratica*

that grew by the rivers of Babylon
where they'd wept, remembering Zion.

He'd compounded an error already made
by the authors of the *Clementine Vulgate*

whose *salicibus*, dative plural of willows,
denoted 'where hanged their lyres'. Thus arose

the myth. The *King James Version* followed suit;
Weeping Willow (as we know it) taking root

in sorrow, instead of its native Northern China.
Dry ground is the preference of *Salix matsudana*

as it should be known. Taxonomists are slow
to correct their antecedents even though

the *New International Version* has caught up:
'There on the poplars we hung our harps.'

When did 'weeping' become the epithet
for trees that cannot bear their own weight?

As if they bent 'to comfort all that mourn.'
As if gravity wasn't the arbiter of form.

Jean Bleakney

THE DYING OF ORPHEUS

the unnatural voices, clamour, the riot
the mother-of-all-bomb shatterings
the self-slapping and furies of the afflicted

the caterwaul as birds of day rip at
birds of night who have wandered out of time

(the tearing jet engines, motor bikes,
the constant drilling and mining and sirens)

bawl against natural consonance,
stutter persistent rhythm
cannot give it ear

—   so that:

        everything gets translated to extremes

        (algae darken the ice-caps, absorb light,
        melt-waters and oceans heighten)

        too much sun, then violent rains
        perish and corrupt the crops,
        rampant darnels and thistles exhaust the land;

        water, which should be shared by all,
        is stolen for some; good air

        (power, gas, light)
        given for the life of all,

is captured for the few

the nursing mother is parched
till her pharynx no longer wheezes into voice

the sun sets the world in all parts
ablaze, a vast furnace

(bush-fires, forest-fires, prairie-fires wild-fires)

flaring air unbreathable
seas and lakes contract,
dust and sand accumulate,
lake-bottoms fissured as deep as Hell
are screened round the world

(reservoirs drain, Italy's
olives and grapes
dessicate on the bough)

till thunder-heads gather again, bolts are thrown,
low fronts and winds unleashed
until all is sea (and tsunamis)
wolves, dolphins, sheep swim
among highest tree branches

(cars and advertising boards swept
along by river-race and overflow)—

beneath all the desire, forefends,
noise, news, tragedy
the singing travels,

groundbass threnody
constant
at the edge of hearing

Steven Matthews

153

SWAM

Across the strait from Thetis Island,
A beach named for shipwrecks,
Curved between the wall of riprap
That edges the booming ground
And the first of the wartime searchlight towers,
Their Cyclops' eyes long out, staring at the ocean.

Log-cluttered tideline, banked shingle,
Foreshore of heaven-strewn rocks, knife-sharp to flesh,
And at one spot, a few yards of weed-free sand,
Never printless for long, soft footing all the way in.

Here, every lunchtime that summer,
You liked to skinny-dip.

>There, once, he caught you by surprise,
>Took you in his arms to kiss,
>And might—the times were different—
>Have fathered a hero on you.
>But you broke loose and he got the message:
>'Either change your own state
>Or let the nymph be who she was before.'

Now it's a clothing-optional beach
With a well marked trail to it.
Four hundred steps down, as many up,
More if you look back.

Mark Vessey

BOOK XII

CYGNUS' POSTCARD FROM TROY

Expect wings.
The earth is tilted.

Homesick,
Your émigrés, your exiles
Come back past—

Falling stars
Out of the night sky,
Or beading
From the distant solar haze,
Ribboning and silver—

Love letters
Landing places

On the shore
On the strand
at Lough Beg.

Maria McManus

THE WAGER

An Archangel bets Beelzebub
she can recover truth
from falsehoods spread
from the House of Rumour—
and Beelzebub, being Beelzebub,
accepts her wager.

At the summit of a great mountain
they find the house Rumour
has chosen for herself—
situated at the centre of the world,
it lies between land, sea and sky,
at the juncture of the tripartite universe,
in a place where all is seen
and heard, no matter the distance.

With countless apertures and entrances,
(it possesses not a single door)
Rumour's house is open day and night and day.
It is constructed of echoing brass
that continually reiterates all it hears.
Rumour's footfall drains her house of silence,
so there is no soundless place, no quiet anywhere within,
just a constant rumbling, like Jupiter making thunder.

At the entrance to Rumour's house,
Beelzebub and the Archangel meet a crush
of idle listeners, and peevish gossips
who mix fact with fiction,
who grow stories

into monstrous beasts with many limbs.

Here are Credulity and Heedless Error,
with Empty Joy and Fearful Consternation;
and here, with Unexpected Treachery,
are Whispers of Uncertain Origin—

Beelzebub makes his way to the Rookery,
where he gathers a truth-full of raven-feathers.
At the dovecote, the Archangel finds
a pity of dove-feathers lying in the dirt.

At the highest rise of Rumour's house,
Beelzebub and the Archangel
release their burden to Wind.
The Archangel claims she can gather every feather
bearing truth, and return it to their sack.

But mischievous Wind snatches the feathers
and molds their shape to a bird,
she teaches the bird flight, breathes voice into it,
but the bird, because of its origins,
can speak only rumour.
It flies about the world, forever out-winging the Archangel.

Rumour, who hears everything, and in her sweep of the world,
misses nothing, observes Beelzebub take devilish pleasure,
and get no pleasure, in winning the wager.

Eleanor Hooker

A SHORT HISTORY OF MYTHOLOGY

To be a lady centaur

        leaping across the Hedgehog Isles

Is to be in heaven

        and wearing a tropical lei

Like a shower of spiral curls

        my tail is springy

It smells like violets and shit

        in a good way

Thank you pool

        I can bounce down a peninsula

Laden with Gorgonzola

        harvesting bites between watching my shows

And inventing the handsaw

        between weaving a tapestry

And visiting space

        I will stomp on a few thousand years

Of lady centaur history

        without regrets

To leap through a waterfall

        in a novelty T-shirt

Holding a gift basket between my teeth

        to shake my legs around

Pretending to be a freaky spider

        to investigate a mole all day

Or whatever is stealing my tomatoes

        is a paradise

Like a partridge

        my head bobs when I run

My boobs bob when I run

        when I run into the purple-tinged hills

I can be mythical
                              like the very specific flower
They use in salads in LA
                                   as a garnish
If you look at it upside down
                              you can see the face of a furious boy

Jane Yeh

THE HOUSE OF RUMOUR

They always tell us it's the centre of earth:
San Francisco: the planet ripping itself apart,
Finding fault everywhere with soil, sea & sky.

Hollywood Bowls: you watch the world go by
Kept under surveillance, hear everything said
Like the old days, gossiping like Louella & Hedda

Spilling on the stars in Beverly Hills. Difference now is
We're the stars & spill on ourselves. Millions
Wi a dozen ways to keep our ears open

& our mouths as well. As one hemisphere tires
& satellites drift, the other comes online, brawling
Sparrows under eaves, constantly bickering.

We can always join in. It's low octane mostly:
The odd time a god condescends to share & 10 million
Acolytes echo instantly against nobodies:

Some farmer shouting at those lonely as herself.
Sure sometimes the Emperor will ban souls to exile
Or the Pontiff broadcast crosswords on sex

& that's news. But as even news proliferates
Our facts get replaced by identical ones
Equally implausible. By the time it's known nobody died

In the fire or 80 or a thousand did, it's too late:
The child's dead already by the time his face
Reaches the screen in the palm of your hand.

Snapchat, Twitter, Facebook, Instagram: the gods
Can't untell their own fabrications & neither can we.
We keep on knitting thread after thread

Till it makes sense but still isn't true.
No one credits what anyone says, no matter who they be.
Even away from the source of the slabbering

We feel the disturbance in the digital force
& have to get to it. What's being said? How many? Where?
'This.' 'I be like.' 'Who knew?' 'Sad.'

The car's still a write-off. Your cappuccino's cold,
iPhone discreetly trembling: a low hum
As if it's the ocean in the shell of your clutch.

That muttering on the bedside table,
A death missed overnight, message waiting.
'Facebook Live or it didn't happen.' It happened. It happened.

Damian Smyth

BOOK XIII

HECUBA BARKS

I

Cassandra foretold these savage times to heedless men.
But even beautiful daughters are not as prized as sons.
I bore nineteen of Priam's fifty boys yet he teased,
'So few!' Made me, daughter of King Dymas, blush.
Might as well discard these royal robes which mock me.
No beauty left. How the Gods disrupt our expectations!
I won't accept a future bonded to Odysseus and Penelope
latched to a loom or weaving in willow, compliant hands and eyes.
Why should I end my days woven in their knots?
Darkening fires still burn our city walls and fields.
Preening Paris brought death inside them when he brought back
the fruit of his desire. To choose from three goddesses
and still hope for a happy outcome! Menelaus sickened for Helen
yet when I looked into her azure eyes I saw only ice.

I was voiceless when Priam bent in supplication before Achilles
to be granted Hector's corpse for proper rites. The coin of exchange
our daughter Polyxena, sacrificed to Achilles's pride. Cut to pieces
    in her
virgin state, her eyes open as the priest's knife struck. How my heart
raged that she would never bear a child. Her father wept when
Polymestor's henchmen put our youngest, Polydorus to the sword.
They filled her brother's goblet again and again under guise
of friendship before they slashed him wildly in a furious dance.
I stopped my tears, took Polymestor's eyes instead. My claws dug deep
to tear him into darkness then cut down his sons with his own lance.
Fury made me fearless. Men assume public space is theirs to keep.

II

You may have heard a rumour of the long ago when Odysseus's boat
heaved homewards with booty on board and me fair game for the
    mockery
of sailors. The God of Gods took pity and set me free—as a dog.
Release and humiliation but not the end of the tale. Granted two
    wishes
by almighty Zeus I became a shape-shifter, a time-traveller.
This is what I am:
the panting dog beside the migrant child,
the knife that slices the belly of the pimp,
the midwife that cleans the blood of the ravished girl,
the unguent that eases the farmworker's limbs as she picks apples
in scalding sun.
This is what I am:
the fingers of the wife beaten to passivity who finds the open door,
the wind blowing dust in the eyes of the honour killer, the drone
that locates the survivors. My work is endless but I do not tire.
I gather strength and purpose as I go.

I am Hecuba, shape-shifter, time-traveller. Hecuba bites.

Hecuba was the wife of King Priam of Troy and the daughter of King Dymas
of Phrygia. After the Greeks burned Troy she was seized by Odysseus to be a slave.
She blinded King Polymestor and killed his two sons to avenge his murder of her
youngest son Polydorus. Her daughter Cassandra had been granted prophetic powers
by Apollo but she was doomed never to be believed. Her youngest daughter Polyxena
was sacrificed to obtain the release of her brother Hector's body from Achilles.

Clairr O'Connor

GALATEA

I

Chisel on stone; his hands shaping her hips. These are her first memories. Next, the slow coming into sound and sense. Her marble home all shatter and shudder after long silence. And then his hand warm between her thighs. She loved him before she learned to speak, loved his hands on her breasts, how he wept against her. Now she knows his rough fumbling, his urgent need. She is learning how to smile; learning how to think at the pace of a human mind. He will never listen slowly enough to match the speed of stone.

II

What is this singing we do? It's no keening in the dark: nations might feel thwarted but we small humans face only sweet challenges: the tilted plough, the bottled lightning. We stitch needlepoint in the nimbus, we swim in uvular tides. We are pebbles, we are only outpost. Not for us the palace fort, the broad sky. If we fly, the air will hold us; if we fall the sea will pay no mind. We have been falling and flying for a thousand years, muddling the coin of our spent breath. We put clay in our mouths to still the wanting. We hold myths in our mouths to keep ourselves safe.

Jen Webb

BOOK XIV

TO TEAR

he was a

'goddess'

'vexed##

fisher of#,

the swollen

waters

sun at his zenith#

scorned

utter of charm.

bring harm

no#

leaf

wort   root

spice   branch

wading to waist

a small weel

banked rise a

soothing bow

she cherished its

calm

the water wheeling at

loin jut part

hounded

brute snout

truth sharp   they maul me, savour blood

from panic to flee

fierce muzzles do tear at me

malicious   smack back, strike! strike again

vicious   they tail, trail

slab tooth   fangs behind snarl

they maul me

at girdle

in circle

me

Monica Carroll

BOOK XV

BEFORE & AFTER

Before

I have been disfigured.
A small white ball has been
Found inside my kidney.
The left one. It's cancer
Says the doctor and we'll
Have to take the kidney
Out. That little marble
Rolls just like the ball that
Spins across a roulette
Wheel. Life's all a gamble
Now and this pearly white
Ball decides my future.
Life or Death. Death or Life.
I have been disfigured.

After

I have been transfigured.
The kidney has come out.
The white ball spins no more—
Seems it came down on Life.
And so I think of my
Transfiguration
Of how I have been changed.
Lesser than I was, but
Greater too in some ways,
As if the ball inside

Me held visions of
An afterlife as clear
As this leftover one.
I feel my heart thump: *Live!*
I have been transfigured.

John O'Donoghue

AUTOSARCOPHAGY FEAST OF HEART,
NUMA'S FIRST SHIELD DISCOVERED IN YASS

Between the double-glaze of French doors
hinging this hour on the past
one, we've sweet-talked our upright vacuum into joining in
on a heist of gods. The band! And, too
it has agreed again to its suction
back through a colander our soul
you know … the kind with enamel and buttercups, blue
how quantum metrology will pack light alive into dark, some fibre
                                                            optic

   christ-
child pork or, at best, scalped and in the end there, acrylic and knit
                                                            orbits

in the round.
  We're nots nowhere near market,
                                        yet … but that armour
is levelling
with a patent office our reason to produce.
                                    A good

less lethal,
  more demand
of sovereign threads. Leverage our bodies,
diacritical macrons stacked and shampooed
as firewood for Romulus hipsters and Etsy
crafters lured by Prussian gold—curlicuing inside the megahertz
our Christian names zip up in. The globalisation of mensch
reaches out   with a Europe of gaffer tape
brands
  the sum'bitch's nozzle onto porous metal?
                                        then gripe
and fumble for bulldogs. Oh, Canberra. We're all out

of fault, and why our Hoover dressed up as your waistline for
                                                              Halloween
is the antlers on undertow and its taxidermy, so
recall, we've baited that fucking thing like a tax haven
and how lingo from Singapore outfoxes
the amortised instruments of Gibraltar's qualm:
albariño or mead? Hurricane design? Now, here's the mark:
cosecant footfalls of twenty-nine
large zoo cats each with curious cheeks and why
they're incising warmth
     out between birch and glass and Etruscan what-have-yous
is zero invention. Later, Shakespearean chorus, say
or the den Grandmaster Flash swung
with shag, they've browsed to bonsaikitten.com and believed
it. Is open. Is yesterday. We're dice and we're whiskers which,
by multiple species—men with pant, without brief, lady's trouser,
                                        a spaghetti of cords and a
dozen shields
angel hair wigs in reverse and, by nomenclature, its beeps—kill.
                                        Rome, if we crouch
on these here *YellowPages*
so that we can spoon your swine frijoles up will we forget our alphabet?
     or have it suck electric clean completely out from us?
won't our name collapse into scrolling numbers?
the weighted mean of them the waste size
of inventors who no longer manufacture Swiss neutrality but invoice
wide afternoons for blowing
on bolognese or the cool embryo of my twin?

Kent MacCarter

173

THE PHOENIX

In the heavens above, on earth below,
everything changes, says Pythagoras,
nothing stays the same. Even we humans,
who are the bearers of immortal souls,
our bodies are made from other bodies
which will die and turn into something else.
All that lives is made from all that has died.

Only one living thing escapes this law,
it gives birth to and dies into itself.
The Assyrians call it the Phoenix.
It does not feed on flesh, nor grass, nor corn,
but lives, as it were, on air, on perfume,
the gum of incense, the sap of balsam.
In this way it lives for five hundred years

until there comes a day it finds itself
drawn to a tall tree. It climbs to the top
and makes a nest for itself, from smooth spikes
of nard, cinnamon, cassia and myrrh.
At last it places itself on the nest
and slowly in that scented place it dies,
its beak and claws unspotted by this world.

Shortly after, they say, a small Phoenix
comes into birth from its father's body.
When old and strong enough it lifts the nest,
the tomb of its father, its own cradle,
and carries it through gently yielding air
to the city of the sun, where it lays
its framework down before the sacred doors.

Perhaps this is a symbolic gesture.
Perhaps he's glad to leave the nest behind
and know that he'll never see it again.
He wants to start a life of his own now—
for hundreds of years this is what he thinks
he's doing, though it is a remote life,
far removed from normal satisfactions.

One day he finds himself drawn to a tree.
Perhaps then he understands his whole life
has been the making of another nest,
an exact replica of his father's.
My life does not end in a blaze of wing—
this is the song we hear the Phoenix sing.
There is no end, there is no beginning.
I cannot change, I cannot change a thing.

Mark Roper

A QUARE FEW THINGS

Over a lifetime, the gods
make many things of you.

I have been a hart, hunted
through the darkening woods.
I was the vanishing point too;
and the heart pierced by arrows,
chambers breached and flooded.

One terrible winter, I was an Iris.
Oh do not assume that bulbs
remember spring and flowering.

I've sat down at a table laid
with the corpse of my child
and been expected to eat.

And I have soared of course,
seen how the world is spread
wide for those who fly. I have
killed with beak and talons
to fill the little gaping throats.

I have asked for the chariot's reins
and set my whole world blazing.

I have been fox and snake and bear.
I have been stone and waterfall.
I have been loved too much and not enough.
I have been split open by the first green shoot.

I have been folded neat and safe inside my shell.
I have been both grit and pearl.
I have been the earth's gold veins,
the aching rift between the continents.

Best was the time of herd, of being
not one alone, feeling the ripple that moved
breath-connected through us; the power
of knowing when to run—before the blow is struck
or the teeth sunk—and when to go back to grazing.

Moyra Donaldson

ALKIONI

I was decades and oceans away
from Vori and Crete
by the time I found that you
—Alkioni—
had given us Halcyon Days:

the unexpected flur of river colours
kingfishering across our eyes
and that rare quiet
you had about you
in the midst of it all.

The mother of my landlord,
you defied your daughter-in-law
and took me on the church trip.
We left at dawn, without
coffee or breakfast

a pilgrimage more daring
and raucous than pious.
The bus drove for hours
into the mountains,
women fighting travel sickness

burying their faces
in handfuls of basil
they worried between their fingers
like rosaries.
You wanted me to see,

specially,
in the Orthodox Monastery,
a miraculous icon of Christ
who opened his eyes
to look at you

or closed them at the sight of you.
We found him
and stood solemn together.
He was charcoal
and pencil.

His eyelids
gradually opened
and he gazed
at us. I
was sore amazed.

As my doubt turned to wonder,
your wonder became disappointment
and disdain—
*Eh! That's just the way
the artist drew it.*

Kate Newmann

179

MERMAID GROWL

for arwuju, Adie Miller (nee Raggett)

Through the sweltering savannah we amble
between shade trees and honeycombed escarpment
           where a faint quiver of thermal plumes
                          is a shape glimpsed riding high
above the rot and vapour of this world:

where an ancient sea bed is upheaved
           and fractured into stratified
blocks, eroding as columns, and conceived
           in this glare as akin
to Angkor's crumbling temple towers, a complex
           lost to rock figs and palms in oppressive
dregs of time:

           but to nana *this strong one country*
is pregnant with Barrawulla whose after-birth
                    is a white and sulphur-crested mineral bleaching
                    and the organ pipe formations
           are Barrawulla's ravenous gouging
                          of a fat country extracting
           Gudanji boring grub remembering:

so at the edges of these crystal clear thermal springs
                    there are cruel curling foams
           and from underwater ledges and crevasses
                          long trailing algae blooms
seem on the cusp of some metamorphosis
           like the larval-nymph dragonfly

in a long past volcanic age:

> but nana reassures me: *it safe to swim, go on.*
> *Nuwalinya are quiet in this place*
> > *Bing Bong long way, they grow wild there*
> > > *with them cheeky fishers*
> *an that port dredgin' devastation:*

> and so I enter the warm mineral-rich waters
> where elsewhere ensnarement trails
> > > silver hair.

Arwuju is Gudanji for 'nana' or grandmother, on your father's side.

Barrawulla is Gudanji for White Cockatoo Dreaming. This particular Dreaming site is at the junction of several Dreaming Trails featuring Jagududgu (the emu) and Barrawulla and is a meeting place where Gudanji and Yanyuwa people come together for ceremony. This ancient area is known by whitefullas as 'The Lost Cities' because of its myriad towering sandstone columns.

Gudanji is one of four surviving Indigenous language groups in the Northern Territory's Gulf of Carpentaria.

Nuwalinya is Indigenous language in the Gulf region of northern Australia for 'mermaid'; perhaps originally a Yanyuwa word, this term is now used widely by most Indigenous people of the Gulf. Nuwalinya are spirits associated with waterways. They perform both a creative and protective function as they roam across Country.

Phillip Hall

THE SILENT RAVEN

The raven is nostalgic for whiteness.
That was its original colour.
Before it chattered a bit too much,
And its snowy white was turned to pure shadow.
Not a metamorphosis, really,
Since the form remained the same.
So what might you say, my classicist,
Metapigmentation or something?
At least it's not a case of metempsychosis
Or the sad psychosis of some of its descendants.
The raven, or the crow, too,
Might have yearned for peacock-like eyes on its wings
That could peer into the secret
Of the multidimensional universe.
But in reality, for no logical reason,
White went black and the world became unfair.
But that world is only Greco-Roman, you know.
In the northern myth of another continent
The raven, cultural hero, brought light to this world
And was at once a human and bird.
I go with the ravens and crows.
Honestly, this black-and-white argument is quite
Moot. If you know how to look at
Their true colour, it's blue.
A blue that transcends night and day,
The old world and the new world,
Life and afterlife.
That's the colour of the sky
And the raven embodies
The fate of the Earth and its atmospheric coating.

This much I learned, *meu deus,* I'd better stop my chattering.
But let me add this one thing: there's another angle to this question.
A true synthesis of black and white is already accomplished
By the magpie. It steals.
A meta-raven, a meta-crow, it globalizes myth with its real-life
    action.
Pied and always on the go,
Aggressive yet very funny,
My cultural hero, my previous and after-life!

Keijiro Suga

FOOTNOTES FOR OVID

Let the day come that rounds off
my uncertain span. The work is done.
                    —Envoi

At the same time, […] the Empire was flooded with ecstatic cults. For all its Augustan stability,
it was at sea in hysteria and despair, at one extreme wallowing in the bottomless appetites and
suffering of the gladiatorial arena, and at the other searching higher and higher for a spiritual
transcendence—which eventually did take form, on the crucifix.
                    —Ted Hughes, introduction to *Tales From Ovid*, 1997

I

Begin, again, at the beginning: how a shower spills
black coins on a warm pavement—smells
of earth's dust rousing and running, beginning to stir
the prow of an olive leaf in a Roman gutter.

II

While the old world slept on the brink of a new star sign,
you orchestrated your song of bodies changed—
clambering, tripping on shadows—into new forms;

incestuous tangle of gods and humans deranged
by passions, bodies and minds a disturbed swarm;
energies dark as the Primal Chaos, galaxies

galloping apart, Earth's blood (a warm embrace
broken for good—how everything in time flees
from itself, for another body, another place,

forsaking its lucky day in the sun to flick
the channel: another spark for the old theme
that is always new as The Odyssey, your lineage, fit

to carry us to the end of the Anthropocene.

III

Exiled for *carmen et error*, whatever the mistake,
you had the last word, *vivam.* Your song escaped,
resurfacing like those dolphins you saw, each lucent,
embodied wave your freewheeling testament.

IV

Call it the Age of Would-Be Giants, days
of nostalgia for 'greatness', 'the people', 'strong' men
chanted into power, as blind to omen
as the weakest emperors, given to Midas-displays—
gold-fevered bathroom fittings, penthouses, lifts—
unable to form one classic thought or settle
longer than it takes to hurl a mountain or piss
that no-longer-precious metal.

V*

Beards whiten. Hair, when shaken, tinkles
with tiny icicles.

The rest of the body cowers as the polar Boreas
whistles and blows The Black Sea into glass.

Walking out onto that slippery roof,
you gauge its solidity, uncracked even by hooves;

looking towards the horizon, note
the absence of dolphins, an ice-anchored boat,

and, below your feet, the fish pent
in windowed cells, some of them breathing yet.

* The final section refashions some images and observations from Frederick Brittain's 'plain prose' translation of a poem by Ovid, 'Exile By The Black Sea', published in *The Penguin Book of Latin Verse* (1962).

Mark Granier

POST-META MOR PHOSIS

an eye of medusa
flew for a while over the manuscript
green rhyming its waves
full of algae.
It was the start of life,
the sounds were wet,
the arch of noah arose from the depths.
around its deck , huge islands swam.
on them, later, in other eras of
the author 's existence,
dreams of glass
stepped in the heads
of the sleeping poets.
near them the sands were mocking
like the hourglass of seas or the huge walls where blind worlds
age their wines
in the dark, under the heat
of a veiled sun, inside the cask of a geologist prospecting his inner
planet.

Florin Dan Prodan

BIOGRAPHICAL NOTES

PATIENCE AGBABI's latest collection is *Telling Tales* (Canongate, 2014), supported by a Canterbury Laureateship and Grant for the Arts to write a contemporary Canterbury Tales. It was shortlisted for the 2014 Ted Hughes Award and Wales Book of the Year 2015.

AMINA ALYAL has published two collections, *The Ordinariness of Parrots* (Stairwell Books 2015) and *Season of Myths* (Wordspace at Indigo Dreams 2016). She teaches creative writing and English literature at Leeds Trinity University.

STEVE ARMSTRONG lives in Newcastle. He won the Bruce Dawe Poetry Prize 2015, has shortlisted for many major prizes. His poems can be found in *Notes for Translators* 2012 (ASM); *Australian Love Poems* (Inkerman & Blunt). He anticipates his first collection will be published in 2018.

CASSANDRA ATHERTON is a prose poet and scholar. She was a Harvard Visiting Scholar in English in 2016 and a Visiting Fellow at Sophia University, Tokyo in 2014. She has published seventeen critical and creative books. Her most recent books of prose poetry are *Trace* (2015), *Exhumed* (2015) and *Pika-Don* (2017).

TONY BARNSTONE teaches at Whittier College and is the author of 18 books and a music CD, *Tokyo's Burning: WWII Songs*. His books of poetry include *Pulp Sonnets*; *Beast in the Apartment*; *Tongue of War: From Pearl Harbor to Nagasaki*; *The Golem of Los Angeles*; *Sad Jazz: Sonnets*; and *Impure*. The editors are grateful to Tupelo Press for permission to publish 'Thing' which first appeared in *Pulp Sonnets* (Tupelo Press 2015)

JEAN BLEAKNEY was born in Newry in 1956. Her *Selected Poems* was published in 2016 and her fourth collection *No Remedy* is due in late 2017, both from Templar Poetry. Her work is studied at GCE Advanced Level in Northern Ireland. She lives in Belfast.

MERLINDA BOBIS, after four novels, has returned to poetry with her new book, *Accidents of Composition* (Spinifex, 2017). In 2016 her novel, *Locust Girl. A Lovesong*, won the Christina Stead Prize for Fiction and the Philippine National Book Award. She continues to dream and write in Canberra.

CHRISTIAN BÖK is the author of *Eunoia* (2001), a bestselling work of experimental literature, which won the Griffin Prize for Poetic Excellence. Bök is a Fellow in the Royal Society of Canada, and he teaches at Charles Darwin University.

189

ROBYN BOLAM's Bloodaxe poetry collections are: *The Peepshow Girl* (1989), *Raiding the Borders* (1996), *New Wings* (2007) and *Hyem* (2017). Other publications include *Eliza's Babes: four centuries of women's poetry in English* (Bloodaxe) and editions of plays by Aphra Behn and John Ford.

KEVIN BROPHY writes fiction, poetry and essays. His latest book is *This is What Gives Us Time* (Gloria SMH 2016). He is a Professor at the University of Melbourne, and now shares his time between Melbourne and the Aboriginal community of Mulan in Western Australia.

DAVID BUTLER's second poetry collection, *All the Barbaric Glass*, was published in March 2017 by Doire Press. He is the recipient of literary prizes for short fiction, drama and poetry.

MAGGIE BUTT has published five poetry collections and a novel. She is an Associate Professor of Creative Writing at Middlesex University where she's taught since 1990, and a Royal Literary Fund Fellow at the University of Kent. Her most recent poetry collection is *Degrees of Twilight* (2015).

ANNE CALDWELL is a freelance writer, a lecturer in creative writing for the Open University and a PhD student of creative writing at the University of Bolton, UK. She is the author of three collections of poetry, the most recent being *Painting the Spiral Staircase* (Cinnamon, 2016).

KIMBERLY CAMPANELLO's poetry books include *Imagines* (New Dublin Press), *Strange Country* (The Dreadful Press), *Consent* (Doire Press) and *Hymn to Kālī* (Eyewear Publishing). *MOTHERBABYHOME* is forthcoming from zimZalla Avant Objects. She is a Lecturer in Creative Writing at York St John University.

SIOBHÁN CAMPBELL's latest book is *Heat Signature* (Seren Press 2017) following *Cross Talk*, *The cold that burns* and *The Permanent Wave*. She holds awards in the National and Troubadour International competitions and won the Oxford Brookes International Poetry Award.

VAHNI CAPILDEO's books include *Utter* (Peepal Tree, 2013), *Simple Complex Shapes* (Shearsman, 2015), and *Measures of Expatriation* (Carcanet; Forward Poetry Prizes Best Collection; T.S. Eliot Prize nomination). She is a Douglas Caster Cultural Fellow at the University of Leeds.

MONICA CARROLL is an experimental writer and poet. Her creative and work has been widely awarded and anthologised within Australia and abroad. Her research interests include phenomenology, artists' books and space. She recently published *Isolator* (2017) with Recent Work Press.

EILEEN CHONG is a Singapore-born Sydney poet. Her books are *Burning Rice* (2012), *Peony* (2014), and *Painting Red Orchids* (2016) from Pitt Street Poetry. *Another Language* (2017) was published in the Braziller Series of Australian Poets in New York, USA.

JANE CLARKE's first collection, *The River*, was published by Bloodaxe Books in 2015. Originally from a farm in Roscommon, she now lives in Wicklow. In 2016 she won the Listowel Writers' Week Poem of the Year Award and the Hennessy Literary Award for Poetry.

KATHARINE COLES's sixth collection of poetry, *Flight*, was published in 2016 by Red Hen Press. Her fifth collection, *The Earth Is Not Flat*, was written under the auspices of the National Science Foundation's Antarctic Artists and Writers Program. She is a Distinguished Professor at the University of Utah.

OLIVER COMINS lives and works in West London. Templar Poetry has published three short collections in the last few years: *Yes to Everything, Staying in Touch* and *Battling Against the Odds.*

STEPHANIE CONN is a poet from Northern Ireland. Her first collection, *The Woman on the Other Side* (Doire Press) was shortlisted for the Shine/Strong Award for best first collection. Her pamphlet *Copeland's Daughter* won the Poetry Business Pamphlet Competition and is published by Smith/Doorstep.

CATHERINE ANN CULLEN has published three collections, including *The Other Now: New and Selected Poems* (Dedalus 2016), and two children's books. She won the 2017 Business to Arts Award for Creativity in the Community for her residency in East Wall, Dublin and is twice winner of the Francis Ledwidge Award.

ENDA COYLE-GREENE was born in Dublin where she still lives. Her first collection, *Snow Negatives*, won the Patrick Kavanagh award in 2006 and was published by the Dedalus Press in 2007. Her most recent collection, *Map of the Last*, also from Dedalus, appeared in 2013.

COLIN DARDIS is a poet and editor based in Belfast. He co-runs Poetry NI, and is editor for Lagan Online. One of Eyewear Publishing's Best New British and Irish Poets 2016, a collection with Eyewear, *the x of y*, is forthcoming in 2018. He is a past recipient of the Artist Career Enhancement Scheme from the Arts Council of Northern Ireland.

KATE DEMPSEY's poetry is widely published in journals in Ireland and the UK including *Poetry Ireland Review* and *Magma*. Prizes include The Plough Prize and commendations for the Patrick Kavanagh Award. A poem from her debut collection, *The Space Between* (Doire Press 2016) was highly commended for the Forward Prize.

MOYRA DONALDSON, from Co Down, has published seven collections of poetry including *Selected Poems* (2012), *The Goose Tree* (2014) from Liberties Press, Dublin and *Abridged 0 -36 Dis-Ease* (2015) a collaboration with photographic artist Victoria J Dean.

KATIE DONOVAN has published five books of poetry, all with Bloodaxe Books. The most recent, *Off Duty* was shortlisted for the 2017 Irish Times/Poetry Now Prize. She is the 2017 recipient of the Lawrence O'Shaughnessy Award for Irish Poetry.

MOIRA EGAN's seventh collection, *Synæsthesium*, won The New Criterion Poetry Prize and will be published by Criterion Books, New York, in Autumn 2017. With her husband, Damiano Abeni, she has published volumes in translation in Italy by authors including Ashbery, Barth, Bender, Ferlinghetti, Hecht, Simic, Strand, and Charles Wright. She lives in Rome.

LUKE FISCHER is a poet, philosopher, and scholar. His books include the poetry collections *A Personal History of Vision* (UWAP Poetry, 2017) and *Paths of Flight* (Black Pepper, 2013) and the monograph *The Poet as Phenomenologist: Rilke and the New Poems* (Bloomsbury, 2015). He is currently co-editing a volume of essays on the philosophical dimensions of Rilke's Sonnets to Orpheus (Oxford University Press).

ANNE FITZGERALD was raised in Sandycove, County Dublin. Her poetry collections are *Swimming Lessons* (2001), *The Map of Everything* (2006) and *Beyond the Sea* (2012). Her fourth collection *Vacant Possession* is forthcoming from Salmon in 2017.

ROSE FLINT is a writer and art therapist. She has published five collections, including *A Prism for the Sun* from Oversteps. Awards include the Cardiff Poetry Prize and the Petra Kenney International Prize.

ANNE-MARIE FYFE's fifth poetry collection is *House of Small Absences* (Seren Books, 2015). Born in Cushendall, Co. Antrim, Ireland, Anne-Marie lives in London where she works as an arts organiser. She has run *Coffee-House Poetry's* readings and classes at London's leading live literature venue, the *Troubadour*, since 1997.

PEGGIE GALLAGHER lives in Sligo. She was shortlisted for Strokestown International and Gregory O'Donoghue poetry awards and was winner of the Listowel Writers' Week Poetry Collection in 2012. Her first collection, *Tilth*, was published by Arlen House in 2013.

TESS GALLAGHER's twelfth volume of poetry, *Is, Is Not*, will be published by Graywolf Press in America in 2019. *Midnight Lantern: New and Selected Poems*, is her most presently complete volume of poetry from Bloodaxe available in Ireland and the UK. She spends time in a cottage on Lough Arrow in Co. Sligo in the West of Ireland, and also lives and writes in her hometown of Port Angeles, Washington.

MARK GRANIER is a Dublin-based writer and photographer. His collections are *Ghostlight* (Salmon Poetry 2017), *Haunt* (Salmon Poetry, 2015), *Fade Street* (Salt, 2010), *The Sky Road* (Salmon, 2007) and *Airborne* (Salmon, 2001). Prizes and awards include The Vincent Buckley Poetry Prize and Patrick and Katherine Kavanagh Fellowships in 2011 and 2017.

PHILIP GROSS has published twenty collections of poetry, including *The Water Table* which won the TS Eliot Prize 2009, and most recently *A Bright Acoustic* (2017). He is a keen collaborator with musicians, other writers and visual artists, e.g. *A Fold In The River* with Valerie Coffin Price (2015).

PHILLIP HALL is a poet and essayist. He lives in Melbourne's Sunshine and his publications include *Sweetened in Coals* and (as editor) *Diwurruwurru: Poetry from the Gulf of Carpentaria*. His chapbook, *Borroloola Class*, was published in the IPSI series this year, and UWAP will publish a new full collection, *Fume*, in February 2018.

OZ HARDWICK is a writer, photographer, music journalist, and occasional musician based in York (UK). He has published six poetry collections, most recently *The House of Ghosts and Mirrors* (Valley Press, 2017). Under the pseudonym of Paul Hardwick, he is Professor of English at Leeds Trinity University.

SUSAN HAWTHORNE is the author of a novel *Dark Matters (*2017), and nine poetry collections including *Lupa and Lamb* (2014) *Limen* (2013) and *Cow* (2011). Susan is the winner of the Penguin Random House Best Achievement in Writing, 2017 Inspire Award and Adjunct Professor at James Cook University, Townsville.

DOMINIQUE HECQ grew up in the French-speaking part of Belgium and now lives in Australia. Her works include a novel, three collections of short stories and five books of poetry. Over the years, her work has been awarded a variety of prizes. *Hush: A Fugue* (UWAP, 2017) is her latest book of lined and prose poetry.

PAUL HETHERINGTON is Professor of Writing in the Faculty of Arts and Design at the University of Canberra, head of the International Poetry Studies Institute (IPSI) there, and co-founding editor of the international online journal *Axon: Creative Explorations*. He has published eleven poetry collections and won the 2014 Western Australian Premier's Book Awards (poetry).

ELEANOR HOOKER's second collection, *A Tug of Blue* (Dedalus Press) was published October 2016. Her first, *The Shadow Owner's Companion* was shortlisted for the Strong/Shine award. She is Programme Curator for Dromineer Literary Festival. She is helm on Lough Derg RNLI Lifeboat.

SUBHASH JAIRETH lives in Canberra. He has published poetry, fiction and nonfiction in English, Hindi and Russian. His publications include three collections of poetry and four books of prose fiction and non-fiction. His book of poetic prose pieces *Incantation* was published in September 2016 (Recent Work Press)

JUDY JOHNSON is co-editor of a 25 year retrospective, *Contemporary Australian Poetry*. She has published six collections. Her verse novel *Jack* won the Victorian Premier's Award. Her latest collection *Dark Convicts* (UWAP, 2017) concerns the life and times of her two ex-slave First Fleet ancestors.

FRED JOHNSTON was born in Belfast in 1951 and educated there and Toronto, Canada. He is the recipient of Hennessy Literary Awards for poetry and prose. He has published eight collections of poetry, four novels and two volumes of short stories. He has received awards from the Arts Council of Northern Ireland and the Arts Council of the Republic. His most recent collection of poems is *Alligator Days*, (Revival Press). He lives in Galway.

KEIJIRO SUGA is a Tokyo-based poet and professor of critical theory at Meiji University's graduate program. He has published four collections of poems under the general title of *Agend'Ars* with the fifth, *Numbers in the Twilight*, to be published in late 2017. His anti-travelogue *Transversal Journeys* (2010) was awarded the Yomiuri Prize for Literature in 2011.

MATT KIRKHAM was born in Luton, and lives and works in Co. Down. His latest collection is *The Dumbo Octopus* (Templar). He has had one pamphlet from Templar, *Aged Fourteen My Grandfather Runs Away To Sea*. *The Lost Museums* (Lagan) won the Strong Prize for best first collection in Ireland.

CATHERINE PHIL MACCARTHY's collections include *The Invisible Threshold* (2012), *Suntrap* (2007), *the blue globe* (1998), *This Hour of the Tide* (1994), and *One Room an Everywhere*, a novel, (2003). She received *The Lawrence O Shaughnessy Award for Irish Poetry* in 2014 and won the Fish International Poetry Prize in 2010. A forthcoming collection, *Daughters of the House*, is due for publication.

PAUL MADDERN was born in Bermuda and has lived in Ireland since 2000. He has three publications with Templar Poetry: *Kelpdings* (2009), *The Beachcomber's Report* (2010 – shortlisted for Shine/Strong Award), and *Pilgrimage* (2017).

STEVEN MATTHEWS is a poet and critic born in Colchester, Essex, UK. Waterloo Press published his first poetry collection, *Skying*, in 2012. A second collection, *On Magnetism*, appears from Two Rivers Press late in 2017, as does *Ceaseless Music*, a creative-critical interaction with Wordsworth's *The Prelude*.

KEVIN PATRICK MCCANN has published seven collections of poems for adults, one for children, a book of ghost stories and *Teach Yourself Self-Publishing* (Hodder) co-written with the playwright Tom Green. He is currently working on a selected poems and a new edition of the ghost stories.

KENT MACCARTER is a writer and editor. He's the author of three poetry collections: *In the Hungry Middle of Here* (Transit Lounge, 2009), *Ribosome Spreadsheet* (Picaro, 2011) and *Sputnik's Cousin* (Transit Lounge, 2014). He is also editor of *Joyful Strains: Making Australia Home* (Affirm Press, 2013), a non-fiction collection of diasporic memoir.

IGGY MCGOVERN is Fellow Emeritus in Physics at Trinity College Dublin; he has published three collections of poetry: *The King of Suburbia* (Dedalus Press 2005), *Safe House* (Dedalus Press 2010) and *A Mystic Dream of 4* (Quaternia Press 2013). A new collection, *The Eyes of Isaac Newton*, is due from Dedalus Press in 2017.

MARIA MCMANUS has written *Available Light*, (Arlen House), and *We are Bone*, *The Cello Suites* and *Reading the Dog* (Lagan Press). Her writing for theatre includes work with Kabosh, TinderBox, Red Lead, Replay, Big Telly and Off the Rails companies. She lives in Belfast.

PAUL MILLS has written five collections of poems published by Carcanet and Smith|Doorstop, and two plays performed at The National Theatre and West Yorkshire Playhouse. His publications also include *Writing in Action* and *The Routledge Creative Writing Coursebook*, and the pamphlet *Out of Deep Time*, Wayleave Press.

GERALDINE MITCHELL, born in Dublin, lives on the Co. Mayo coast, overlooking Clare Island. She has published three collections of poetry, *World Without Maps* (Arlen House, 2011) and *Of Birds and Bones* (Arlen House, 2014) and *Mountains for Breakfast* (Arlen House, 2017). She won the Patrick Kavanagh Poetry Award in 2008.

DAVID MORLEY won the Ted Hughes Award for New Poetry in 2016 for *The Invisible Gift: Selected Poems* and a Cholmondeley Award for his contribution to poetry. A Professor at Warwick University and Monash University, David is also a National Teaching Fellow.

GRAHAM MORT has published nine full-length collections of poetry and also writes BBC radio drama and short fiction. His first collection of poems, *A Country on Fire*, won a major Eric Gregory Award. He has also been awarded the Bridport Prize for short fiction and the Edge Hill Prize for his book of stories, *Touch*. His latest poetry book, *Cusp*, appeared in 2011.

PAUL MUNDEN is Postdoctoral Research Fellow (Poetry & Creative Practice) at the University of Canberra, and Director of the UK's National Association of Writers in Education (NAWE). He has published five collections including *Analogue/ Digital: New & Selected Poems* (Smith|Doorstop, 2015) and *Chromatic* (UWAP, 2017).

KATE NEWMANN worked for a year in Crete at the Museum of Ethnology. She has compiled the *Dictionary of Ulster Biography* as well as fourteen community books, and has published four collections of poetry, with a fifth, *Ask Me Next Saturday*, due this winter. She is co-director of the Summer Palace Press.

DOIREANN NÍ GHRÍOFA is a bilingual writer (in Irish and English). Among her awards are the Rooney Prize for Irish Literature. She frequently participates in cross-disciplinary collaborations, fusing poetry with film, dance, music, and visual art. She is an Associate of the Trinity College Centre for Literary Translation, Dublin.

JEAN O'BRIEN's fifth collection, a new & selected, entitled *Fish on a Bicycle,* was published by Salmon publishing in 2016. She has won, amongst others, the Arvon International and the Fish International poetry prize.

CLAIRR O' CONNOR is author of two novels, *Belonging* (Attic Press 1991) and *Love in Another Room* (Marino 1995). Her poetry collections are: *When You Need Them* (Salmon), *Breast*, *Trick the Lock*, *So Far* and *Caesura*, *New and Selected Poems*, all with Astrolabe Press.

MARY O'DONNELL was born in Monaghan and lives in Kildare. Poet, short story writer, and novelist, her seventh collection, *Those April Fevers*, appeared in 2015. Fiction includes the novel *Where They Lie*. and *The Elysium Testament*. Her debut novel, *The Light-Makers* (1992) was re-issued by 451 Editions during 2017.

JOHN O'DONNELL's work has been published and broadcast widely. Awards include the Irish National Poetry Prize, the Ireland Funds Prize and a Hennessy Award for Poetry, as well as a Hennessy Award for Fiction. He has published three poetry collections. His *New and Selected Poems* is forthcoming from Dedalus Press in 2018.

JOHN O'DONOGHUE is the author of *Sectioned: A Life Interrupted* (John Murray, 2009); *Brunch Poems* (Waterloo Press, 2009); and *Fools & Mad* (Waterloo Press, 2014). *Sectioned: A Life Interrupted* was awarded Mind Book Of The Year 2010.

NESSA O'MAHONY was born in Dublin and lives there. She has published four books: *Bar Talk*, appeared (1999), *Trapping a Ghost* (2005), *In Sight of Home* (2009) and *Her Father's Daughter* (2014). She is co-editor with Siobhán Campbell of *Eavan Boland: Inside History* and presents The Attic Sessions, a monthly literary podcast.

MAEVE O'SULLIVAN is the author of three collections from Alba Publishing (UK): *Initial Response* (2011), *Vocal Chords* (2014) and *A Train Hurtles West* (2015). A fourth travel-themed collection, *Elsewhere*, is forthcoming from Alba.

ALVIN PANG is a poet, writer and editor from Singapore. He is a board member of the University of Canberra's International Poetry Studies Institute and a doctoral candidate in the practice of creative writing with RMIT University. His latest book is *What Happened: Poems 1997-2017*.

PAULINE PLUMMER is an Irish/Welsh mix from Liverpool but has lived in North East UK since the 80s. She has several collections of poetry, most recently, *Bint* (Red Squirrel Press 2011), a novella in verse *From Here to Timbuktu* (Smokestack 2012). Her collection of short stories *Dancing With a Stranger* was published in 2015 (Red Squirrel Press).

FLORIN DAN PRODAN (b. 1976) is the founder of the literature and art group *Zidul de Hârtie* from Suceava. As a poet he has published *On the Road. Poeme de călătorie,* Shambhala Press, Kathmandu, Nepal, 2012, *Poem pentru Ulrike*, Vinea, Bucharest, 2013, *Poeme şi note informative,* Zidul de Hârtie, Suceava, 2014. He is an editor of the magazine *Bucovina literară.*

CRAIG RAINE has written six books of poetry, two novels, three books of critical essays, and is the editor of *Areté.* His verse play *1953* was directed by Patrick Marber at the Almeida Theatre in 1996 and his opera libretto *The Electrification of the Soviet Union* was performed at Glyndebourne, Berlin and Wuppertal in 1986. His study, *T S Eliot*, was published in 2007. His latest book, *My Grandmother's Glass Eye: A Look at Poetry* appeared in 2016.

PAISLEY REKDAL is the author of five books of poetry, most recently *Imaginary Vessels* (Copper Canyon, 2016). A former Guggenheim and NEA fellow, she is the current Poet Laureate for the State of Utah.

NELL REGAN's third collection is *One Still Thing* (Enitharmon Press, 2014). Awards include an Arts Council Literature Bursary and the Patrick and Katherine Kavanagh Fellowship. Her latest publication is the biography *Helena Molony A Radical Life* 1883–1967 (Arlen House, 2017). She lives in Dublin.

MARK ROPER's latest collection is *Bindweed*, Dedalus Press, Autumn 2017. *A Gather of Shadow*, Dedalus 2012, was shortlisted for The Irish Times Poetry Now Award in 2013 and won the Michael Hartnett Award in 2014. He has collaborated on 2 publications with photographer Paddy Dwan.

MILES SALTER's collections include *The Border* (Valley Press, 2011) and *Animals* (Valley Press, 2013), and he co-edited the *Valley Press Anthology of Yorkshire Poetry* (2017). He was Director of York Literature Festival between 2009 and 2016.

JOHN W. SEXTON is the author of five poetry collections, the most recent being *The Offspring of the Moon (*Salmon Poetry, 2013). His sixth collection, *Futures Pass*, is forthcoming from Salmon in 2018. In 2007 he was awarded a Patrick and Katherine Kavanagh Fellowship in Poetry.

RAVI SHANKAR is the author, editor or translator of over a dozen books, including most recently *The Golden Shovel: New Poems Honoring Gwendolyn Brooks* (University of Arkansas Press, 2017) and *Andal: The Autobiography of A Goddess* (Zubaan Books/ University of Chicago Press, 2016). He has won a Pushcart Prize, a Glenna Luschei

Award from Prairie Schooner and been awarded many fellowships. He founded *Drunken Boat*, one of the world's oldest electronic journals of the arts.

PETER SIRR has published ten collections with Gallery Press, most recently *Sway* (2016), versions of poems from the troubadour tradition. *The Rooms* (2014) was shortlisted for the Irish Times Poetry Now Award and the Pigott Poetry Prize. *The Thing Is* (2009) was awarded the Michael Hartnett Prize in 2011. *Black Wreath*, a novel for children, was published in 2014. He lives in Dublin and is a member of Aosdána.

MELINDA SMITH is the author of five books, most recently *Goodbye, Cruel* (Pitt St Poetry, 2017). Her previous book, *Drag down to unlock or place an emergency call*, won the 2014 Australian Prime Minister's Literary Award for poetry. She is based in the capital city Canberra and is a former poetry editor of *The Canberra Times*.

ELIZABETH SMITHER's latest collection of poems, *Night Horse*, was published earlier this year by Auckland University Press. She was New Zealand poet laureate (2001-3) and received the Prime Minister's Award for Literary Achievement in Poetry in 2008.

DAMIAN SMYTH's five collections are *Downpatrick Races* (2000), *The Down Recorder* (2004), *Lamentations* (2010), *Market Street* (2010) and *Mesopotamia* (2014). *English Street* is due in 2018. He is Head of Literature & Drama at the Arts Council of Northern Ireland.

SHANE STRANGE lives in Canberra. His writing has appeared in various print and on line journals, including *Overland, Griffith Review, Burley* and *Verity La*. He teaches at the University of Canberra.

GEORGE SZIRTES is a poet and translator. Born in Hungary in 1948, he published his first book of poems, *The Slant Door*, in 1979. It won the Faber Prize. Has published many since then, *Reel* (2004) winning the T S Eliot Prize, for which he has been twice shortlisted since. His latest book is *Mapping the Delta* (Bloodaxe 2016).

DAVID TAIT's first collection *Self-Portrait with The Happiness* was shortlisted for The Fenton Aldeburgh First Collection Prize and received an Eric Gregory Award. He lives in Nanjing where he works as an English teacher. His new collection *The AQI* is forthcoming from Smith|Doorstop.

GRÁINNE TOBIN lives in Newcastle, Co Down. Her books are *Banjaxed* and *The Nervous Flyer's Companion* (Summer Palace).

CSILLA TOLDY's poetry collection *Red Roots - Orange Sky* was published by Lapwing Publications Belfast in 2013, followed by an anthology of short fiction, poetry and memoir titled *The Emigrant Woman's Tale* in 2015.

JESSICA TRAYNOR's debut collection, *Liffey Swim* (Dedalus Press), was shortlisted for the 2015 Strong/Shine Award. In 2017, a sequence of poems in response to Jonathan Swift's *A Modest Proposal* was published by The Salvage Press.

MARK TREDINNICK—whose books include *Almost Everything I Know*, *Bluewren Cantos*, *Fire Diary*, *The Blue Plateau*, and *The Little Red Writing Book*—is a poet, essayist, and writing teacher. Two new poetry collections, *Walking Underwater* and *A Beginner's Guide*, will be published in 2018

MARK VESSEY grew up in England and has for many years taught literature and history at the University of British Columbia (Vancouver), where he is currently Principal of Green College. His publications include essays on Jerome, Augustine, Cassiodorus, Donne and Derrida. He is the editor of *Erasmus on Interpretation and Representation in Literature and Theology*, due in 2019 from the University of Toronto Press.

BREDA WALL RYAN lives in Bray, Co Wicklow. Language, nature and mythology inspire her poetry which has been widely published, translated and broadcast. Among her awards are The Dromineer, Over the Edge New Writer, iYeats, and Gregory O'Donoghue International Poetry Prizes. Her first collection *In a Hare's Eye* (Doire Press) won the Shine/Strong Award 2016.

JEN WEBB works at the University of Canberra. She is ACT editor of the *Australian Book Review*'s States of Poetry annual anthology, and co-editor of the bilingual anthology *Open Windows: Contemporary Australian Poetry*. She is also the author of several poetry chapbooks, and—with Paul Hetherington—of *Watching the World: Impressions of Canberra*.

GRACE WELLS' debut poetry collection, *When God Has Been Called Away to Greater Things* (Dedalus Press, 2010), won the Rupert and Eithne Strong Award and was shortlisted for the London Festival Fringe New Poetry Award. Her second collection is *Fur* (Dedalus Press, 2015).

NERYS WILLIAMS, originally from West Wales, lectures in American Literature at University College, Dublin and is a Fulbright Alumnus. Her volume *Sound Archive* (Seren:, 2011) won the Strong first volume prize in 2012. Her second volume *Cabaret* (2017) is available from New Dublin Press.

ANTHONY WILSON is a poet, writing tutor, blogger and Senior Lecturer at the Graduate School of Education, University of Exeter. His most recent books are *Lifesaving Poems* (Bloodaxe, 2015), *Riddance* (Worple Press, 2012) and *Love for Now* (Impress Books, 2012).

JOSEPH WOODS is an Irish poet whose Tomis is Harare, Zimbabwe and previously Rangoon, Burma. A fourth collection *Monsoon Diaries* is forthcoming with Dedalus Press.

MÁIRÍDE WOODS writes poetry and short stories. Her work has appeared in anthologies and reviews and on RTE radio. Two poetry collections, *The Lost Roundness of the World* and *Unobserved Moments of Change*, have been published by Astrolabe. *A Constant Elsewhere of the Mind* appeared in October 2017. Máiríde lives in North Dublin.

ENDA WYLEY has published five collections of poetry, most recently *Borrowed Space, New and Selected Poems*, Dedalus Press, 2014. She was the inaugural winner of the Vincent Buckley Poetry Prize, Australia and the recipient of a Patrick and Katherine Kavanagh Fellowship, 2014. She is a member of Aosdána.

JANE YEH is a Lecturer in Creative Writing at the Open University. Her first collection, *Marabou* (Carcanet, 2005), was shortlisted for the Whitbread, Forward, and Aldeburgh poetry prizes in the UK. She was named a Next Generation poet by the Poetry Book Society for her second collection, *The Ninjas* (Carcanet, 2012).

2016 Editions

Pulse **Prose Poetry Project**
Incantations **Subhash Jaireth**
Transit **Niloofar Fanaiyan**
Gallery of Antique Art **Paul Hetherington**
Sentences from the Archive **Jen Webb**
River's Edge **Owen Bullock**

2017 Editions

A Song, the World to Come **Miranda Lello**
Cities: Ten Poets, Ten Cities **Various**
The Bulmer Murder **Paul Munden**
Dew and Broken Glass **Penny Drysdale**
Members Only **Melinda Smith** and **Caren Florance**
the future, un-imagine **Angela Gardner** and **Caren Florance**
Tract **Prose Poetry Project**
Poet to Poet: Contemporary Women's Poetry from Japan **Various**
Proof **Maggie Shapley**
Black Tulips **Moya Pacey**
Soap **Charlotte Guest**
Isolator **Monica Carroll**
Íkaros **Paul Hetherington**
Metamorphic: 21st Century Poets Respond to Ovid **Various**
Work & Play **Owen Bullock**

all titles available from

www.recentworkpress.com

RECENT
WORK
PRESS

CPSIA information can be obtained
at www.ICGtesting.com
Printed in the USA
LVOW12s2117131217
559598LV00006B/815/P